Side by Side

Learning to Share and Bear Life's Burdens

Brenda Barnes Poarch

Publishing Designs, Inc.

P. O. Box 3241

Huntsville, Alabama 35810

Cover and page design: CrosslinCreative.net
Images: ClassicStock.com, CreativeMarket.com, iStock.com, VectorStock.com

Cover photos by Celine Sparks Photography

Editors: Peggy Coulter, Debra G. Wright

Printed in the United States of America

Publisher's Cataloging-in-Publication Data

Poarch, Brenda Barnes, 1956

pp.: 144

Includes chapters and study questions.

1. Strength in Trials 2. Group Networking 3. Mentoring

1. Poarch, Brenda Barnes

2. Title

ISBN 978-1-945127-09-0

248.8

To Peggy Shipp Walker

Even though her side-by-side walk with me was very brief, Peggy Walker changed the course of my life. It was Peggy who encouraged me to begin writing these Bible lessons. She would not take no for an answer or allow me to use fear or self-doubt as an excuse. But most of all, Peggy demonstrated through her own life that even illness should not stop you from serving the Lord.

Peggy has since succumbed to her lifelong suffering and is now with the Lord. However, her spirit, love, and dedication to God live on in those of us who knew and loved her. I look forward to meeting her in heaven and saying thank you. Until then, I am fully committed to walking side by side with God and my fellow Christian sisters!

Endorsements

Brenda Poarch's use of scripture, humor, and sound common sense makes her readers come away with practical everyday application of God's word. Her insightful questions promote study, thought, and communication. *Side by Side* is for any woman of any age, race, education, or social status who seeks a better relationship with God and His people!

—Beverly McEldowney, Middleburg, Florida

Brenda's teachings include easy to follow, down to earth, real-life discussions about problems that Christian women face every day. Brenda covers very difficult subjects that need to be discussed without stepping on toes.

—Adena Parker, Combine, Texas

Brenda Poarch's classes are both motivating and inspirational. I felt secure in sharing private thoughts and feelings which allowed for a much greater degree of introspection. I thoroughly enjoyed the author's ability to speak to women's everyday issues in a practical way and relate modern matters to teachings of the Bible. It is refreshing to see that many Christian women face the same issues and have the same concerns I do.

—Diane Perdue, Myrtle Beach, North Carolina

Brenda Poarch's writing is uplifting and encouraging. She helped us examine and evaluate our own lives. We were able to face personal discussions in a relaxed and risk-free environment, sharing our own experiences with each other. We developed personal bonds. Most of the conversations were issues that women deal with in everyday life. We realized that the answer to our problems were right there in the Bible. She is right to the point.

—Nedre White, Phoenix, Arizona

Contents

PART 3

PART 4

PART 5

Introduction

W e've all been there. Life is great, things are going well, and then seemingly out of nowhere the storms hit. What's a sister to do during emotional, financial, spiritual, or physical hurricanes? Pack a storm survival kit, of course!

Just like those on the coast pack a hurricane survival kit, you and your group will pack a life-storm survival kit. Storms are not so bad when you are prepared. After all, it is not *if* a storm will come, but *when* the storm will come. Are you ready for the storms of life? Soon you will be. Part 1 of *Side by Side* helps us survive "Through All Kinds of Weather."

"Chronic Illness" is a storm that certainly calls for your survival kit, as well as your side-by-side sisters. These mortal bodies are difficult to live with when they're malfunctioning, but you certainly can't live without them. How will you respond when faced with a day-to-day struggle of pain and uncertainty? When Jesus described the judgment scene, He talked about the sick. Maybe we should too! I know all too well how life can change in an instant. Many illnesses come and go, but what about disease that decides to take up residence in your body? Not your problem? Maybe not, but one day it might be. Besides, you certainly know someone who suffers like that, right? Will you be the one who stands by her side? Look for answers in the section, "When Abnormal Becomes Normal."

Physical illness isn't the only plaguing storm. Many women struggle with their emotions. As Christians, we sometimes think that negative emotions are a sign of weak faith or ingratitude. One of the greatest prophets of God struggled emotionally. It's not a sin or a lack of faith! Some of my sisters have a chemical imbalance beyond their control. Many of us, however, are wounded mentally from life's battles. How can we help a sister who is struggling emotionally? Do we need to ask for help if we are the ones struggling? We will examine how God the Father took care of one of His own in his afflictions. Through scripture and the wisdom of the side-by-side women in your class, you will visualize hope and appreciate real life, practical solutions. These issues are uncovered in the section, "Lions, Tigers, and Bears—Oh My!"

You will need your in-the-trenches buddies for "The Sin No One Confesses" section, because you'll tackle the storm of sin, particularly, one sin that no one has ever confessed. Yes, it's true! You can look through scriptures, talk to friends, or even ask your preacher. No one has ever repented of this sin. How is that possible? What is this secret sin? If you really want to know, don't miss participating in this section. I think you will be surprised by the answer. It is near the end of the book for a reason. You know what they say, *Go big or go home!* So, I'm going big! Please join me.

When you have finished this course, you will be richer—not in dollars, but in friendships. *Side by Side* can then become your reference of survival for the next storm. Put on your cap and gown and celebrate not only what you have learned but the sisters and brothers you have strengthened as well.

God's family is the best support system in the world. When we do it God's way, blessings flow beyond our wildest dreams, and some of the best blessings will be sitting right there in the room beside you. It is pure joy for me to take this journey with you. God loves you and so do I.

Pledge

I, _____ do hereby pledge to begin each Bible study with prayer.

I will ask God to open my heart to the suffering and struggles of others, to give me courage to admit my own faults, to ask for help, and to keep anything I hear during these classes in the strictest of confidence.

I pledge not only to give advice but also to take it.

I pledge to seek out the counsel of an older person and to give respect to those women who have walked the path before me.

I pledge to do all of these things humbly and in a manner that gives glory to God.

Signed: _____

Date: _____

♪♪ Side by Side ♫

Oh! we ain't got a barrel of money,
Maybe we're ragged and funny,
But we'll travel along, singin' a song,
Side by side.

Don't know what's comin' tomorrow,
Maybe it's trouble and sorrow,
But we'll travel the road, sharin' our load,
Side by side.

Through all kinds of weather,
What if the sky should fall?
Just as long as we're together,
It doesn't matter at all.

When they've all had their quarrels and parted,
We'll be the same as we started,
Just travelin' along, singin' a song,
Side by side.

—Harry Woods, 1927

PART 1

Through All Kinds of Weather

SURVIVAL

Singing Side by Side
Pat, Phyllis, and Becky

Sometimes sorrow and tragedy produce lifetime friendships. But singing kept our threesome side-by-side. Singing was the greatest joy of the Banks Sisters: Pat, Phyllis, and Becky—that's me.

We were dubbed "The Lemon Sisters" because we sounded just like the Lennon Sisters but with more sour notes. We sang for ladies' functions, teas, and weddings. We loved learning new songs, thinking up fun programs, practicing, and performing! Pat often said, "We have the same nasal cavities!" "Side by Side" was a favorite.

Our lives were not problem-free. When we were challenged, we'd prod each other toward more Bible study. Not only did we sing and study together, but we were also speakers. Once all three of us shared lessons at the Yosemite Ladies Retreat, where we stayed up till all hours of the night, talking, laughing, reminiscing, and sharing Bible insights.

But Phyllis started having trouble catching her breath when she got tickled, and we were frightened. We tried (unsuccessfully) to curtail our laughter, and we shortened our practices. Eventually she was diagnosed with interstitial lung disease.

We sang another two and a half years after her last hospitalization, accompanied by her oxygen supply. We sang for a ladies' day March 2017, and for a birthday party in April. We had no earthly idea that she would only be with us another week.

Although Pat and I feel the loss of our third part so keenly, our trio has become a duet, "traveling along, singing a song, side by side."

—Becky Bullough, California

Storm Alert: When, Not If

In the day of prosperity be joyful, but in the day of adversity consider: Surely God has appointed the one as well as the other.

—Ecclesiastes 7:14

♪♫ Song ♫

Peace, Be Still

Pledge

I do hereby pledge to begin each Bible study with prayer.

I will ask God to open my heart to the suffering and struggles of others, to give me courage to admit my own faults, to ask for help, and to keep anything I hear during these classes in the strictest of confidence.

I pledge not only to give advice but also to take it.

I pledge to seek out the counsel of an older person and to give respect to those women who have walked the path before me.

I pledge to do all of these things humbly and in a manner that gives glory to God.

Growing up in Florida, hurricanes were never frightening. At the beginning of the hurricane season, we simply put our kit together and waited. Most years we never needed the supplies, but on rare occasions we did. The meteorologists would tell us when a storm was going to arrive, how long it would last, and how strong it would be. If the storm was predicted to be intense, we evacuated, but most of the time a hurricane meant a day off from school and, for some, a hurricane party. It was an exciting adventure!

So in 2005 when we were told that a fierce lady named Katrina was approaching New Orleans, I laughed at my concerned Mississippi neighbors. After all, my roots were in Florida. I was an expert on hurricanes. Besides, we were living "way up north" near Jackson, Mississippi, hundreds of miles from the coast—or so I thought. There was no way we would be affected by this storm. Only afterward did I look at a map. That "hundreds of miles" from New Orleans to Jackson? One hundred fifty-eight miles!

But now, let's get back to the storm and my fantasies about the safety of my community.

No Way? Really?

As I stood behind the ironing board in my living room watching the coverage of the devastation caused by Katrina in New Orleans, I began to reconsider my bravado. Could I be wrong? Was there really a need for concern this far from shore? My questions were abruptly answered by a loud pop and a sudden power outage. Now the storm had my attention! I called my husband and begged him to come home. Without the news to distract me, my living room window became my view of the world, and there was a real storm raging outside.

We scrambled for flashlights and batteries and fretted about the food in the fridge. This Floridian was not prepared! It was a long, dark, hot, frightening night. When the morning light came, Katrina was still a force to be reckoned with. There were trees down, some roof damage, part of the privacy fence demolished, and debris everywhere. Katrina had clearly left her mark.

For the next three days, life revolved around simple basics: food, water, ice to preserve perishables, and waiting. We were among the few blessed to have power restored quickly. After three long days we celebrated the privilege to live comfortably again. Cool air, a hot bath, clean clothes, and food from the kitchen! Things I once took for granted now seemed like great blessings. Finally, the storm was over and life would return to normal. At least, that is what I thought.

Forgive Me When I Whine

A friend called me to ask a favor. She explained that she had family coming up from the coast and was running out of room in her home. She had no power, but they were fine. She could take care of the family already there, but could I please take in a family of four? "Of course," I said. "I am thrilled to do it." I quickly prepared my home and waited for the family to arrive. I will never forget the day these precious people showed up on our doorstep. As the mother, father, and two middle-school children began to explain what the last few days had been like for them, I was humbled and ashamed of my complaining.

Running from the storm, their life was truly about survival. The luxuries of physical comfort or food were not a concern for this family. They were just trying to stay alive. High winds, torrential rain, mass flooding, downed power lines, falling trees, and darkness created constant life-threatening conditions. They had heeded the warnings and evacuated miles from home, only to realize that they had not gone far enough. The home to which they had evacuated was still in an area devastated by the storm. After several days of living with a group in a crowded hot home with no power and little water and food, they decided to venture farther north.

The displaced family was exhausted, but happy to be someplace they actually felt safe. Once their pressing physical needs were met, they gathered before the television to see the disastrous effects Katrina had brought to the community they had left five days earlier. They thought they were prepared to witness the results of the storm, but nothing could have prepared them for the horrific devastation presented by the newscasters.

My heart raced as we turned on the TV. Wanting to be as close as possible to the pictures, they refused to sit on the furniture, but instead took places on the floor directly in front of our antiquated 19-inch TV. As the cameras panned the area, they shouted out the identity of familiar landmarks. "I travel that road every day on my way to work." "My friends live down that road." "That tall building in the background, that's where I work." "Show us the school!" they begged the TV set. And then, "What about our neighborhood?"

Silence filled the room as pictures of the Superdome, screaming rooftop survivors, and lifeless bodies lying in the mud streamed across the TV screen. The pain was raw and palpable. How could this have happened? Could New Orleans ever recover from such a devastating storm? What about their home, their school, shops, and places of business they frequented? What about their friends, co-workers, and family? For almost an hour we sat in silence watching the videos of death, destruction, and despair. This storm I had mocked had taken the lives of many and changed forever the lives of all who had managed to survive.

I came to love and respect that brave family. I wish I could have done more to ease their pain and suffering. They only stayed a day or so. They thanked us and returned home as soon as word reached them that the roads to their community had been cleared. They were anxious to return to New Orleans to see what was left of their home and the city they loved.

I couldn't watch it on TV. It was all just too sad!
—Sister Sidekick

❋ What's the greatest natural disaster you have experienced?

_____

❋ Did you know it was coming? Were you prepared?

_____

❋ How did you survive?

_____

_____

❋ Write your probable daily activities in each of the three columns below:

Day Before Disaster   Day of Disaster   Day After Disaster

_____   _____   _____

_____   _____   _____

_____   _____   _____

❋ When Lot was escorted from Sodom just in time to escape the fire and brimstone, what treasured possessions went with him?

_____

Hurricane in the Heart

Hurricanes, tornados, floods, and blizzards frighten us with both physical and emotional destruction. Most of us will experience at least one major storm in our lifetime and some of us will endure many more. At best, a storm will mean a disruption in routine and some mild inconveniences. At worst, as in Katrina, these tragedies bring death and destruction.

When calamity strikes, we not only deal with a natural disaster but an emotional one as well. We might be able to avoid a natural storm, such as a hurricane, by choosing where we live, but emotional storms can come at any time in any place. Heart storms are normal reactions to difficult events. Health crises, deaths, financial struggles, divorces, relocations, and job changes are just a few examples of potential disasters. Often we cannot prevent the "heart" attacks, but I believe we can prepare for them.

> Beloved, do not think it strange concerning the fiery trial which is to try you, as though some strange thing happened to you (1 Peter 4:12).

Storms are coming. It is not a matter of *if* but *when.* Let's compare heart storms with hurricanes. As mentioned at the beginning of the chapter, I packed a hurricane survival kit every year at the beginning of hurricane season. If a survival kit serves a valid purpose, why not pack one for emotional storms?

Imagine yourself placing a large plastic box on the table. On one side of the plastic tub there is a sign that reads Mary's Storm Supplies, or whatever your name is. Now open the lid and look inside. Is anything there? No? How is that a problem? Can you possibly expect to survive a storm if you have absolutely no supplies?

Caregiving Women

Women are often drafted to become experts in preparing to take care of family and friends. How many people have you assured, "I'll be there for you, no matter what"? How many times have you given up something you wanted to help someone else?

If you looked in the survival kits of your loved ones, would you find them abounding with reinforcements that you placed in there to help them survive? Probably. However, after all this giving, women sometimes neglect themselves, and when a storm hits, they find there is absolutely nothing in their own supply kit. Am I right?

Let's get real about surviving life's storms. If we are going to outlast our disasters, we must be prepared. Let's pack our survival kits: Get those tubs out and begin packing supplies to fortify our spirits.

Weather-Proof Survival

Remember our lesson theme for the week is "Storm Alert: *When, Not If.*" It is the first of three lessons that will increase our awareness of the need for personal survival in uncertain weather. In these three lessons, each of us will make a personal "Side-by-Side Survival Kit."

We'll place five items in our kits: A storm tracker journal, emergency contacts, supplies, a flashlight, and a communication device. These are physical symbols of spiritual fortification.

Journal. A hurricane storm tracker is a booklet that explains hurricanes and how they form. It provides a map with a grid, so you can track your hurricane.

What should your storm tracker look like? A journal is the logical choice because it's the best tracker. Get a book that suits you to use as a journal. The size, shape, or look is not important. You are just looking for a safe place to write your thoughts. Remember, this is your preparation for survival.

✸ In the front cover of your journal, write the following text:

> To everything there is a season,
> A time for every purpose under heaven:
> A time to be born, and a time to die;
> A time to plant, and a time to pluck what is planted;
> A time to kill, and a time to heal;
> A time to break down, and a time to build up;
> A time to weep, and a time to laugh;

> A time to mourn, and a time to dance;
> A time to cast away stones, and a time to gather
>   stones;
> A time to embrace, and a time to refrain from
>   embracing;
> A time to gain, and a time to lose;
> A time to keep, and a time to throw away;
> A time to tear, and a time to sew;
> A time to keep silence, and a time to speak;
> A time to love, and a time to hate;
> A time of war, and a time of peace.
>   —Ecclesiastes 3:1–8

Solomon's words remind us that life is about change, and change of any kind can result in a storm.

❀ On the back cover of your journal write: *He makes His sun rise on the evil and on the good, and sends rain on the just and on the unjust* (Matthew 5:45). Jesus is reminding you that just because your neighbor is being blessed and you are suffering does not mean God loves your neighbor more than He loves you.

Next, go through your journal and write your favorite encouraging scriptures. Sprinkle them throughout the journal, little surprises on each page. Be creative. You can use different colored ink, writing styles, and even throw in a few stickers or pictures if you are inclined. Date the journal and place it into your kit along with a few ink pens.

Good News, Bad News

Hurricane season lasts just a few months out of the year, and it directly affects only those who live near the ocean. However, life's storms can come at any time and in every place. Why would I point out something so obvious? Did you notice that in Ecclesiastes 3:1–8, for every positive event there is a negative one? We expect storms when the news is bad, but we are often caught off guard by the storms that good news can bring.

For example, there is a time to be born and a time to die. We expect a storm when a loved one dies. We expect it and therefore we are not surprised by it. But what about a storm when a baby is born? Young mothers are often unprepared for the emotional storm that comes as a result of bringing a new baby into the family. I have even seen cases where her support system is less than supportive because they do not understand why she would have any negative emotions associated with this blessed event. Have you ever been there?

The fact of the matter is, anytime there is a major change in our lives, that change can bring about a storm. So your storm tracker is not necessarily looking only for storms but for changes in the weather pattern of your life. This knowledge cannot prevent the storm, but it will increase your chances of survival and help you to feel less vulnerable and more in control.

Why?

A storm tracker also explains why. We've all heard the weatherman speak of fronts, barometric pressure, system highs and lows, and the jet stream. Although I don't fully comprehend everything being said, there is something very comforting about hearing the why.

When struggling through the storms of life we often ask why. Sometimes there is a clear answer, but many times we suffer simply because we live in an imperfect world with imperfect bodies. Oh, there may be times we can link our suffering to bad decisions or even sin, but Jesus tells us in Matthew 5:45 that God sends both rain and sun to all people, both good and bad. Satan would love for us to feel abandoned or even punished by God when we suffer. Please don't let hard times separate you from the love of God. He is our only hope.

Write It Down

When the storm comes, you will be ready. You now have a safe place to express yourself. Don't hold back saying what is on your heart. Many of us suffer terribly because we feel reluctant to express our thoughts. Remember, this journal is for your eyes only. Are you afraid God will be mad if you write it down? Really? Do you seriously think God does not already know what you are thinking? I reckon if He knows how many hairs you have, He knows you are struggling emotionally.

❋ What other things could you include in your journal that would make it more beneficial during difficult times?

_____

_____

Get Real with God

God is tough. He can take it. I am not suggesting that you curse or deny Him, but I am asking you to come clean about your emotional struggles, fears, and desires. It is perfectly all right to ask God why and tell Him that you are angry, afraid, or feeling alone and discouraged. If we cannot tell our Father what is on our hearts, who can we tell?

By writing down what we are thinking and feeling, we can track our emotions. Kept inside, our feelings will swirl and churn like a storm, but if we get them out onto paper, we can see the size of the storm and project its course. Be honest. Don't be afraid to ask yourself the tough questions: What do I really feel?" "Why do I feel this way?" "Is there anything I can do to reduce my suffering?"

By expressing yourself on paper and then reading what you have written, you can not only see where you are emotionally but also where you have been and how God brought you through that storm.

The Israelites may not have written down the story of God's deliverance from every calamity, but they did create physical memorials. That was not only to remind eyewitnesses of God's provisions but also to instill this truth on future generations.

* Read Joshua 4:1–9 and brainstorm ways that we can do the same using the journal in our survival kit.

Please remember that God loved us enough to send Christ to save us. Don't let a storm separate you from the love and blessings of God. Once you have purged your emotions you can begin to deal with them. We all need a safe place to vent, and you are taking action by creating a journal for that purpose.

There are four more items we will discuss for your kits in the next two weeks. But for now, please discuss the questions below. This is a fun lesson. The point here is to be prepared for *when, not if*.

* Why do many women put themselves last? Is this a biblical principle? Why or why not? Discuss times when putting yourself last is not practical. (Example: Airline emergency instructions.)

---

* Work on setting up your journal as suggested. Share the main thoughts and scriptures you feel will benefit you and your sisters.

* Why do some women need to talk about their problems more than others do?

✳ What type of woman are you—talkative or quiet about your life storms?

_____

✳ Examine the event of Peter sinking in the sea (Matthew 14:29–31). Observe how he coped with his storm by writing below.

How did he respond?

_____

_____

What helped him?

_____

_____

What else might have helped him?

_____

_____

Pack for Trouble and Sorrow

The pains of death surrounded me, and the pangs of Sheol laid hold of me; I found trouble and sorrow. Then I called upon the name of the Lord: "O Lord, I implore You, deliver my soul!"

—Psalm 116:3–4

♪♪ Song ♫

A Shelter in the Time of Storm

Pledge

I do hereby pledge to begin each Bible study with prayer.

I will ask God to open my heart to the suffering and struggles of others, to give me courage to admit my own faults, to ask for help, and to keep anything I hear during these classes in the strictest of confidence.

I pledge not only to give advice but also to take it.

I pledge to seek out the counsel of an older person and to give respect to those women who have walked the path before me.

I pledge to do all of these things humbly and in a manner that gives glory to God.

Last week we established our "Side-by-Side Survival Kit." No matter who you are or where you live, storms are coming.

Each of us placed one item in our kits, a journal as our storm tracker. Today we will continue the process of being prepared for the storms of life.

- ✓ 1. Storm Tracker Journal
- ☐ 2. Emergency Contacts
- ☐ 3. Supplies
- ☐ 4. Flashlight
- ☐ 5. Communication Device

I'm ready, let's start packing! Hey, does this raincoat make me look fat? —Sister Sidekick

Emergency Contacts

There was a time when I could rattle off all my important numbers from memory. Today, between old age and my cell phone directory, I have very few numbers floating around up there. My hurricane kit needs to contain a list of telephone numbers of important people and places. That includes my family, doctor's office, bank, pharmacy, church, and anyone I might need in case of a crisis. My memory died a long time ago and cell phones go dead, so it is important to have these numbers in writing.

Write Names and Numbers

You need a list of emergency contact numbers for your side-by-side survival kit. Spend some time in prayer. Then take a 3x5 card and make a list of the names and phone numbers of the people you can trust and those who have shown capability to endure storms. Your list may not include your best friend, husband, or a family member. In fact, those closest to you sometimes are not the best people for this role because of their emotional attachment to you. You are actually looking for mature people who have the "been there, done that" T-shirt.

Once you have completed your list, ask to meet with each of your contacts in private. Tell them you are preparing for life's storms, and ask if you could come and talk to them if your storm becomes too great for you to bear alone. Most acquaintances are honored to be asked. Remember, you want a Christian for this role, because you will need godly advice.

Write Inspiring Scripture

Write the verses below on your card to remind you that giving and receiving love, support, and help is not an arbitrary choice; it is a commandment. Do not feel guilty about applying these scriptures. Asking for help is not a sign of weakness but of wisdom. You are wise because you are using the support system God intended for you when He created the church. If you have other applicable verses, include them too. Once your card is complete, place it inside your kit.

- *Galatians 6:2.* Bear one another's burdens, and so fulfill the law of Christ.

- *John 13:34.* A new commandment I give to you, that you love one another; as I have loved you, that you also love one another.

- *Romans 12:15.* Rejoice with those who rejoice, and weep with those who weep.

Guidelines for Sharing Secrets

I am blessed to have a couple of friends in whom I can confide. My best friend and I have been sharing each other's secrets for more than thirty years. If you have such a friend and want to have a similar relationship with her, the guidelines we use might be beneficial to you.

- *You are not allowed to talk.* When listening to a sister vent about one of her loved ones, you may listen, but you may not add to what she is saying in a negative light. She is venting and most of what she says will be emotional, not factual. She just needs a safe place to say how she feels at that moment. Once she has calmed down, she may not remember what she said about her loved one, but she will remember what you said. And that might not be good.

- *You are not allowed to change your opinion of the loved one based on this new information.* When we are angry or hurt, we will paint the offending person in the most damaging light possible. After the storm is over, facts may change slightly or soften. In her anger, you are hearing only one side of the story. Try to keep your emotions in check. Later you can decide how you feel. Right now it is all about her.

- *You may not heavily defend the offending person or situation right now.* If you believe the information is inaccurate, you may offer facts; however, be certain that you do so calmly and softly. Please remember you are dealing with someone in the midst of a storm. Now is not the time to try to defend. Once your sister has finished venting and has some time to digest the actions of the offending party, she will be more receptive to the facts. Right now she is hurting and just needs a place to express her pain.

- *You are not allowed to repeat any information you have received unless given permission.* The only exception to this rule would be if there is eminent danger. Otherwise, my sisters, keep your mouth shut (Proverbs 11:13).

- *You are not to give advice unless asked.* Just because a hurting sister shares her story with you does not mean she expects you to solve her problem. She may only need you to listen. If she does ask for advice, be gentle. Share stories of triumph over similar situations, not defeat, especially if she is dealing with a health crisis or some other life-altering event. Always remind a hurting sister of God's love and His awesome power to overcome anything this world throws our way.

• *You are not to judge.* If you and your friend agree that you can serve each other as an emergency contact person, you must also agree that you are not there to judge one another. We have all done and said things we regret. Our survival kits contain emergency contact numbers so that if we are in a crisis we have someone to call for help. You will not get a lecture from the ER doctor before he treats you and neither should you get a lecture from a friend.

> Therefore be merciful, just as your Father also is merciful. Judge not, and you shall not be judged. Condemn not, and you shall not be condemned. Forgive, and you will be forgiven. Give, and it will be given to you: good measure, pressed down, shaken together, and running over will be put into your bosom. For with the same measure that you use, it will be measured back to you (Luke 6:36–38).

The bottom line is to listen. Be a safe place to allow the sister to work through her feelings. How can a person in a crisis know what is truly troubling her until all of her emotions are on the table for examination? The process of being able to safely verbalize is valuable in calming an emotional storm.

So then, my beloved brethren, let every man be swift to hear, slow to speak, slow to wrath.

—James 1:19

But I give such good advice! When do I get to tell my friend what to do? —Sister Sidekick

❋ How can being a safe place to vent show the love of Christ?

Compassion, Go about doing good

❋ Can everyone serve in this way? Why or why not?

❋ If you do not feel you could serve in this way, would you be able to tell someone no?

"SIDE-BY-SIDE" SURVIVAL KIT

Supplies. A good hurricane kit contains necessities: a gallon of water per day per person, canned or boxed foods that can be eaten without cooking, and a basic first aid kit.

Our survival kit can cover all of these areas with just one small book, the Bible. Often in the midst of the storm we forget to feed our souls. Expressing ourselves through journals and talking to good friends is very helpful during the storms of life, but it is the power of God through His word that will keep us alive. To say that we do not need to be constantly in the word, especially during difficult times, would be to say that we do not need to eat today because we ate yesterday.

Choose a Bible that is easy to read and one you can carry with you. Life storms do not always happen at home, and Bibles in print don't need chargers. You might even want a Bible that you have highlighted or inserted margin notes to remind you of studies or inspirations that have helped you in the past. Once you have chosen that "perfect Bible," place it in the kit.

❋ In the scriptures below, Jesus refers to both the bread of life and living water. What does He mean by those terms? Was He saying that Christians would not need to eat or drink? Read the verses below and write in your own words the message being taught by Christ.

John 6:35

_____

_____

John 4:9–14

_____

_____

❋ Christ is called the Great Physician. Why? Write your favorite example of Christ's healing power below. Don't forget to include your verses for reference and later study.

_____

_____

_____

Lean on the word of God when there is a storm in your life. Where will you find greater power and wisdom? Often in our personal storms we are called to make difficult decisions and deal with issues we do not feel capable of handling. God created the heavens and the earth and He has the answers. We must seek them.

If any of you lacks wisdom, let him ask of God, who gives to all liberally and without reproach, and it will be given to him.
—James 1:5

Journal, Cards, Bible. Got it!
What's next? —Sister Sidekick

"SIDE-BY-SIDE"
SURVIVAL
KIT

Flashlight. No hurricane survival kit would be complete without a good source of light. Even those diehard Floridians who never pack a kit will at least make sure they have a working flashlight and a few extra batteries when a storm is approaching. There is something about darkness that frightens even the bravest among us. Without light, we find ourselves stumbling along, groping to feel anything to give us a sense of our location.

Our emotional storm kit must have light as well. The shadows of disaster are deep and can make us feel we are in darkness, alone—afraid and lost. We need a light to guide us, protect us, and reassure us that we are loved and everything is going to be well with us. For a Christian woman, that light is Jesus Christ, the Son of God (John 8:12).

The Light in Your Soul

In the midst of the storm we must hold fast to the Savior. Christ came to earth and lived inside a mortal body. When you say to Jesus, "I'm tired. I'm lonely. I'm afraid. I'm in pain. I feel abandoned. Please let this cup pass," He knows. He understands. He has been there. He has been tired and felt pain. He sweated drops like blood through stress. He felt abandoned on the cross.

I'm not talking about Christ giving off a physical light. I am referring to the light that He can place within our souls that will give us the strength and courage to keep going, to reach out for help when we are lost, hurting, or afraid (Philippians 4:13).

You cannot actually place Jesus in your kit, but you can buy a cute flashlight. Take a Sharpie and write Philippians 4:13 on the side of the flashlight. If there is room, write the whole verse. If not, write the verse on a 3x5 card and the scriptural reference on your flashlight. Either way, I want this verse to give you strength and remind you of the power found in Christ. Once you have done this, place the flashlight in your kit.

- He is the light you will use to write in your journal.

- He is the light you will use to see your contact numbers.

- He is the light you will use to read your Bible.

Pretty amazing, huh? We cannot use anything we have placed in our kits without Christ. There is a message here, one that I know is not lost on you. Without Christ all is vain. Without Him, survival is not possible. God knew that. That is why He sent Jesus. We understand it too, but it never hurts to be reminded.

Prepare to share with your classmates the storm you fear the most. There is probably one type of storm that you feel would totally destroy you. Once you have confessed your deepest fear, reexamine the items you have placed in your kit. How will these items help you face that one big storm?

Remember, your kit-packing is incomplete. Keep turning pages for confidence. You can do this, alongside your sisters.

John 6:35
John 4:9-14
James 1:5
John 8:12

Bonding over Bullies

Iva, Dana, and Sandy

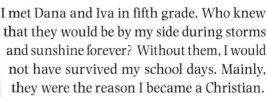

I met Dana and Iva in fifth grade. Who knew that they would be by my side during storms and sunshine forever? Without them, I would not have survived my school days. Mainly, they were the reason I became a Christian.

Proverbs 18:24 says, "A man of many companions may come to ruin, but there is a friend who sticks closer than a brother." That was Dana and Iva—they stuck close to me despite the "many companions" of ruin we three had during junior high. Each day of school was full of anxiety and fear. A group of bullies caused a lot of misery for a lot of students, and we were three of the victims. We never knew when one of us would be called an ugly name or find a hateful note on her desk. We were vigilant for tacks in our chairs; we hid our lunch money in our shoes and kept all of our belongings in our lockers. At school, we wouldn't go to the bathroom all day for fear of being beaten up.

Outside of school was different. In the summer we had slumber parties, became candy stripers together, and went to the movies. Then one summer, Dana and Iva invited me to church, and we participated in the youth group. We went on campfire cookouts, church picnics, and holiday parties.

Eventually we were all baptized at the Toledo Road Church of Christ. As the angel Clarence observed in *It's a Wonderful Life*: "Strange, isn't it? Each man's life touches so many other lives." Because of one invitation I became a Christian, followed by my sister and my parents. I married a Christian man; we have two Christian children. What would my life be like today without those two friends?

Despite the bullies, we made it through school days, and are still close friends. We cherish our ongoing friendship and take comfort in the assurance that we'll always walk side-by-side.

—Sandy Turpin, Ohio

Sharing Our Load

Cast your burden on the Lord, and He shall sustain you;
He shall never permit the righteous to be moved.

—Psalm 55:22

♪♫ Song ♫

Tell It to Jesus

Pledge

I do hereby pledge to begin each Bible study with prayer. I will ask God to open my heart to the suffering and struggles of others, to give me courage to admit my own faults, to ask for help, and to keep anything I hear during these classes in the strictest of confidence.

I pledge not only to give advice but also to take it.

I pledge to seek out the counsel of an older person and to give respect to those women who have walked the path before me.

I pledge to do all of these things humbly and in a manner that gives glory to God.

Are you ready to put the *calm* in calamity? Did it rain in your life since the last lesson? I think I will take a wild guess here and say yes! Of course it did. In fact, many of us probably had severe weather warnings several times throughout the week. Perhaps it was not a category 5 hurricane, but even if it were, hopefully you were more prepared than you were before we began this study.

Let's get real: Storms are a part of everyday life. While some may be larger than others, they will happen. This is Planet Earth. We have not arrived in heaven yet. As long as we are in these mortal bodies, in a world where Satan has power and men are imperfect, Sista, it's gonna rain! We cannot prevent the catastrophes, but we can prepare for them.

It rained on me three times last week . . . and that was just on Monday! —Sister Sidekick

Check Your Kit

Look at your survival kit. So far you should have four items.

☑ 1. *A Storm Tracker Journal*—A cute journal filled with your favorite uplifting scriptures; a safe place to express and record your thoughts.

☑ 2. *An Emergency Contact List*—3x5 cards with the names and numbers of Christian sisters ready to listen.

☑ 3. *Supplies*—Your Bible.

☑ 4. *Flashlight*—Your physical reminder of Jesus.

Now you are ready to add the fifth and final item.

"SIDE-BY-SIDE" SURVIVAL KIT

A Communication Device—Prayer. Before cell phones, ham radios were often the only way to communicate with the outside world after a catastrophic storm. Today many of us would simply charge our cell phones in preparation for an upcoming hurricane; however, communication towers can become overloaded and cell phone batteries die, so the ham radio is still widely used.

Ham radio operators are often regular people who have a love for radios and use them just because they enjoy the hobby. When a storm strikes, these "normal Joes" become heroes. They are able to send calls for help, get important messages to loved ones far away, and receive important messages that save lives. Why? They can do it because they have been using that communication skill all along. They know what to do because they have done it many times before when there was not a storm or a crisis.

Is anyone among you suffering? Let him pray.
—James 5:13

Prayer is our communication device. Like ham radio operators, we should be praying long before a storm or crisis occurs just because we enjoy it. Talking to God in prayer is an awesome blessing we have been given because Christ died for us, tearing the veil and giving us direct access to God the Father. If we have spent our lives in prayer, we will be ready when calamity strikes. We can use our practiced skill to pray for ourselves, and for others. Prayer is powerful. God answers prayer.

And whatever things you ask in prayer, believing, you will receive.
—Matthew 21:22

My Prayer

We want to place something in our kits to remind us to pray. I have given this much thought. Most of the time, prayer is easy for those who love God and speak to Him often. However, there will be those days, especially in the midst of the storm, when we are just too weary to pray. Let's prepare to pray every day.

 Find some really pretty stationery. On the top of one of the pages write "My Prayer." Next, search your heart and list the things for which you are thankful for and write them down. This can be done in paragraph or list form. Once the list is complete, fold the paper and place it in an envelope. On the outside of the envelope write "My Blessings." Place the envelope inside your kit.

> *Be anxious for nothing, but in everything by prayer and supplication, with thanksgiving, let your requests be made known to God.*
> —Philippians 4:6

On the days that the storm threatens to overtake you and you struggle to find the words or the strength to pray, read your list. If possible, read it out loud. You will be amazed at the strength that comes from counting your blessings.

What Is in Your Hand?

Congratulations! You are now ready for any storm. Double check your Side-by-Side Survival Kit now.

☑ 1. *A Storm Tracker*—A cute journal filled with your favorite uplifting scriptures; a safe place to express and record your thoughts.

☑ 2. *An Emergency Contact List*—3x5 cards with the names and numbers of Christian sisters ready to listen.

✓ 3. *Supplies*—Your Bible.

✓ 4. *Flashlight*— Your physical reminder of Jesus.

✓ 5. *A Communication Device*—Your imagery of prayer.

When Words Won't Come

I intentionally saved prayer for last because it is our lifeline to God—a source of strength, help, and hope. Yes, God already knows what we need, but He wants us to ask (Matthew 7:7). However, there will be those days when not even a reminder to pray will help. Are we unable to speak to God if we cannot pray? No, God has that handled too.

Likewise the Spirit also helps in our weaknesses. For we do not know what we should pray for as we ought, but the Spirit Himself makes intercession for us with groanings which cannot be uttered.

—Romans 8:26

Did you see that? Even if you don't know what to say, the Holy Spirit knows your needs. He will make intercession for you. So sisters, please pray when you are weak and pray when you are strong. Pray on the good days and pray through the storms. God is faithful. Even if you are in deep despair and suffering tremendous pain, please pray. Just like the hero on the other end of a ham radio signal, God will hear your pleas and come to your rescue.

Seek out praying Christian sisters. Keep repeating, "Prayer is powerful!" Pray by phone, in person, text messages, emails, or even private Facebook messages. The important thing is to pray.

I love talking to God. You can talk as long as you want to and He never interrupts or falls asleep. Awesome! —Sister Sidekick

Yes, you will have a load. But I am here to encourage you to share your load. Be prepared; pack your kit. However, no matter how difficult the storm, God can raise up something beautiful from the destruction. It may take years to see the good that He produces from the evil that threatened to overtake us, but God is faithful and will deliver.

> *And we know that all things work together for good to those who love God, to those who are the called according to His purpose.*
>
> —Romans 8:28

Hang in there, my sistas. God loves you and so do I. If you are in a storm, please reach out for help. If you know someone who is going through a storm, offer your hand and your friendship. I pray that you will support one another through all the storms of life.

We are the family of God, side by side. It was never His intent for us to endure our storms alone. Just know that one day the storm will pass, and the sun will come out. There will be a rainbow to remind us of God's love and His faithful promises. Together as sisters, with God's help and love, we can weather any storm.

❋ What other items would you put into your kit and why?

❋ Is it possible to pack a kit for another person? How?

_____

_____

❋ Can you help a sister who is going through a storm that you have never experienced? How?

_____

_____

❋ Why do some people seem to live in a storm-filled life, while others have clear skies?

_____

_____

❋ If your life has been virtually trouble free, does it make it harder to relate to those who seem always to be struggling? Explain.

_____

_____

❋ What's the best advice you have received while going through a storm?

_____

_____

PART 2

When Abnormal Becomes Normal

CHRONIC ILLNESS

Side by Side in Strength and Service
Beverly and Millie

We were two busy young mothers who met in the church. What did we have in common? Husbands, children, three-meals-a-day, school activities—along with the joy of Christian sisterhood. After our children were grown, the two of us and our husbands spent a lot of time together as a fun foursome. We worked together serving the Lord in our local congregation, taught Bible classes, ate in each other's' homes, talked, sang, laughed, and cried together. Beverly and I have now been friends for more than 40 years. More importantly, we are sisters in the Lord.

In 1993 Beverly and her husband, Keith, were right by my side when my husband, Dick, became ill and passed away. A few years later when Keith passed away, I supported Beverly.

Since that time, our friendship has been a rock of strength as we adjust to a new chapter in our lives. We still serve the Lord together in our local congregation. Instead of the "fun foursome," we are now the "terrific twosome." Each year we attend a conference in Wichita, where a Christian sister lovingly dubbed us as "The Bobbsey Twins," We often visit the sick and elderly together, prepare and serve meals for the bereaved, talk, sing, laugh, and cry together. I thank God for giving me Beverly as my "side by side" friend!

—Millie Shipp, Kansas

The "Still Suffering" among Us

This is my comfort in my affliction, for Your word has given me life.

—Psalm 119:50

♪♪ Song ♫

Farther Along

Pledge

I do hereby pledge to begin each Bible study with prayer.

I will ask God to open my heart to the suffering and struggles of others, to give me courage to admit my own faults, to ask for help, and to keep anything I hear during these classes in the strictest of confidence.

I pledge not only to give advice but also to take it.

I pledge to seek out the counsel of an older person and to give respect to those women who have walked the path before me.

I pledge to do all of these things humbly and in a manner that gives glory to God.

Prior to 2006, my health history was pretty boring. Other than a breast cancer fight in 1999 and a gall bladder removal a few years later, I did not have much to put on a health history form. Boring, predictable, average—that was me. I wasn't plagued by colds, usually missed the seasonal stomach flu, and could count on feeling good most of the time. My occasional illnesses were short lived and easily cured.

Looking back, I now realize that I took great pride in that fact. I was young, strong, and healthy, and deep down I truly believed that I was the master of my own body. If I wanted to do something badly enough, I could push through the pain and illness and "Git-R-Done!" Even during my yearlong battle with breast cancer, I worked and cared for my husband and kids most of the time. Looking back, it seems like a small bump in the road compared to what I was about to experience!"

Superwoman Lost Her Cape

In 2006, my husband and I moved back to our childhood area of northeast Florida. We bought a house and began major renovations. Then my health began to crumble. At first, I thought it was a stomach bug. Then came the diagnosis of salmonella poisoning, but my bizarre set of debilitating symptoms persisted long after the infection was gone. In just a matter of a few short months, I went from flying Superwoman to bedridden Kryptonite girl. I was afraid and in constant pain.

That began the ordeal to find an answer to my suffering. Along the way I would fight a new kind of cancer, be hospitalized with bismuth poisoning, have shingles, suffer temporary cardiomyopathy (heart failure), and endure the sensations of an irregular heartbeat, all while battling major GI issues and pain. I lost more than seventy pounds, fought depression and panic attacks, and spent most days just trying to survive.

What a difficult time. However, a strange thing happened along the way. Life did not stand still. In the first six agonizing years, my oldest daughter graduated from law school, passed the bar exam, and began her career as an attorney. My middle daughter graduated from college, married, and moved to Florida and then to Texas. My son graduated from college one weekend and married the next. My mother died of pancreatic cancer, and a year and a half later my 81-year-old dad remarried and only spent part of the year near me in Florida, and the rest of his time in Alabama. Life moved on.

Enduring Happy Occasions

I like things to be in order, preferring to have one major thing finished before I begin another. I would have preferred to be well, feeling good, strong, and on top of things before I climbed those milestone-mountains. I never dreamed happy events such as weddings and graduations would become obstacles to endure, instead of events to enjoy and celebrate. It was not in my plan to be so sick. I was not able to minister to my dying mother but, instead, had to depend on others to do my part.

I wanted—no, needed—time to stand still. I just wanted to get my feet on the ground and find my balance before life moved forward without me. These experiences were significant highlights.

I had looked forward to these graduations and marriages from the time my children were born. I had made promises to my mother to care for her in her time of need. That's why we returned to Florida in the first place, to care for aging parents. I wanted to support my dad in his time of grieving and later to celebrate the love and happiness he had found. I could do none of those things. All I could do was survive. I smiled. I participated. I did what I could, but all the while my mind was screaming, "This is not how it was supposed to be!" I want my "normal" back!

Goodbye, Normal

Sadly, many of you know exactly what I am talking about. Your story may be different from mine, but the outcome is the same: abnormal has become your normal. It may be caused by death, illness, accident, divorce, incarceration, catastrophic life events, or relocation. Whatever the cause, the life you envisioned, planned for, and felt comfortable in is now gone. Ripped from your grasp were all control, security, and predictability. At one time you may have felt that life was fair and reasonable, and you were the master of your own ship, but not today. Today is about survival.

Some of you will have no idea what I am talking about. Your normal is still very normal. It may not always be that way, but normal is where you are today. If you find yourself in that place, I believe you just might be at a disadvantage. Great wisdom is developed from difficult life events. Please be open and willing to learn from those ladies in the room who are willing to share their stories with you. I suspect one day you will be very glad you did.

✳ What does *normal* mean to you? How do you decide what is normal and what is abnormal?

_____

_____

✳ Is it possible for one person's normal to be another's abnormal? Why or why not?

_____

_____

✳ How do your personal expectations play a role in what you consider to be normal or abnormal?

_____

_____

Support System

Regardless of where this lesson finds us today, God has a message for all of us. If the church is to be the support system God intended, we must look to the scriptures for guidance. Consider the following eye-opening text.

> And He will set the sheep on His right hand, but the goats on the left. Then the King will say to those on His right hand, "Come, you blessed of My Father, inherit the kingdom prepared for you from the foundation of the world: for I was hungry and you gave Me food; I was thirsty and you gave Me drink; I was a stranger and you took Me in; I was naked and you clothed Me; I was sick and you visited Me; I was in prison and you came to Me" (Matthew 25:33–36).

In this excerpt from the judgment scene, the sheep were being congratulated for their service and love for others. Don't you want to be a part of that crowd? Don't you dream of one day standing before the Father and hearing Him say, "Well done"?

Most Christian sisters are great when it comes to serving the hurting. We can whip up a casserole and get it to a hurting family in a flash. I've been in churches where women would actually fight over getting to do good deeds for the suffering. We form committees, post sign-up sheets, create phone trees, and participate in card ministries. Some churches even have clothes closets, food pantries, and prison ministries.

Long-Term Neediness

We are great at taking care of those in need, or are we? I think the answer to that question is yes and no. We *are* great on the front end. When a new crisis arises, we are Johnny-on-the-spot. However, how many of us (myself included) can write down all the names on the shut-in list?

How many times have we visited or helped someone whose needs are long-term or unchanging? I'm not trying to make us feel bad. I just want us to think. Right now in your group, take a moment to see who can name every person on the long-term sick and shut-in list. I know you have one. All churches do. Sadly, these are the forgotten folks among us. Why? Their abnormal has become normal.

When they first began to struggle, it's likely that there was a lot of support, but now we have become used to their absence. Did we stop looking for them? Did we stop missing them? Did we stop reaching out to them? Probably. Sistas, this ought not so to be.

Forgotten! I haven't forgotten anyone. Give me that pen and paper. Let's see, there's sister Jones and brother Smith and, hmmm, I know there's more . . . —Sister Sidekick

Why? Why do we let this happen? We are not bad people. We care about the hurting. So why is it that when someone has a new need we are all over it, but if the need is long-term or difficult to understand, we drop the ball or roll it the other way?

Regardless of the *why*, let's get real about long-term needs with solutions. This is not an easy subject, but it is certainly necessary because abnormal lingering illnesses are not disappearing. How sobering to know that when we stand before the throne, we will be judged on all we have done and all we have neglected to do.

Consider one Bible event that demonstrates man's reaction to long-term illness. Read Mark 10:46–52 and answer the questions.

✳ What was wrong with Bartimaeus?

_____

✳ Why was he sitting beside the road?

_____

✸ What was the lifestyle of a disabled person in that day and time? How desperate was his situation?

_____

_____

✸ When he began to call to Jesus for help, what was the reaction of those nearby? Why?

_____

_____

> And when he heard that it was Jesus of Nazareth, he began to cry out and say, "Jesus, Son of David, have mercy on me!" Then many warned him to be quiet; but he cried out all the more, "Son of David, have mercy on me!" (Mark 10:47–48).

Shhh! Be Quiet!

When Mark 10:46–52 is preached, the focus is almost always on the man's faith and Jesus' mercy. But why don't we look at the crowd?

Many of these men had just received instruction from Jesus that the greatest among them was to be a servant (Mark 10:43). Yet when a desperate blind man calls out to Jesus for help, they try to silence him. Why?

In scriptures like these, it is very easy to sit back in judgment. We weren't there. But we know how the story ends. We push back our shoulders, puff out our chest, and proclaim how foolish and sinful those people were.

Do well-meaning sisters speculate as to what they would have done if they had been there? Sometimes. Most of us want to feel we would have done the right thing, but would we?

How are we doing with our "Bartimaeus" today?

* In Jesus' day, disability meant a lifetime of suffering and begging. Who in your congregation has long-term needs they cannot meet alone?

* Bartimaeus spent his days begging for the basic necessities of life. No one looked to the future and offered help to prevent his need for begging. Should the physically struggling in your local church have to request everything they need? How might help be offered before a request is made?

* Bartimaeus's needs were legitimate. There was no concern that he was lazy, a fake, or mishandling his funds. In fact, Jesus' followers might have known his family (Mark 10:46). However, when he cried out for help, they tried to silence him. How does your congregation determine who to help and how often? How is that information passed on to those needing help or to those willing and able to help?

Let Someone Else Do It

Now I realize that some who read this will want to pass the burden on to the elders and deacons. Let's get real, ladies. We don't need established programs in order to serve. Our knowledge, compassion, and statistics regarding the needs of others frequently motivate the leadership to organize a program.

I am not suggesting that a church can meet the needs of everyone in the congregation. Sometimes the leaders say no. However, as my momma used to say, "It's not what you say, but how you say it." Remember, we are not examining Jesus' actions. He was perfect. It's the actions and the attitudes of those traveling with Him that are under scrutiny. They believed they truly understood Christ's teaching and yet they tried to silence Bartimaeus. Are we guilty of telling the suffering, "Be quiet"?

Bear one another's burdens, and so fulfill the law of Christ.

—Galatians 6:2

Is it possible that we have become overwhelmed with the needs of the long-term sufferers? Could it be that for all of our quoting of "let us not grow weary while doing good" (Galatians 6:9) that we have become weary? Or worse, is it possible that we have hardened our hearts to the suffering around us without even realizing it? Maybe, or perhaps there is something happening here that has come about so slowly we did not even realize it was happening.

In the next chapter, we will discuss a few issues that contribute to our response to the chronic sufferer.

Pull out your journal and write at least two scriptures from this "Abnormal" lesson. Include any other thought that will help you weather your future storms.

✤ Take out your list of the homebound and chronic sufferers in your congregation and divide them among your class members. See what information you can gather on these "Bartimaeuses" within the next two weeks. You cannot minister to the hurting when you don't know their needs. Begin now to pray for each one daily.

I'll take the first group. I wonder what I can find out! —Sister Sidekick

Does "Why" Matter at All?

He sets on high those who are lowly, and those
who mourn are lifted to safety.

—Job 5:11

♪♪ Song ♫

Does Jesus Care?

Pledge

I do hereby pledge to begin each Bible study with prayer.

I will ask God to open my heart to the suffering and struggles of others, to give me courage to admit my own faults, to ask for help, and to keep anything I hear during these classes in the strictest of confidence.

I pledge not only to give advice but also to take it.

I pledge to seek out the counsel of an older person and to give respect to those women who have walked the path before me.

I pledge to do all of these things humbly and in a manner that gives glory to God.

Were you surprised by what you discovered in the last lesson? If you were not able to complete your research about the chronic sufferers in the local church, don't worry. You have one more week before you will need to use that information. If you did some fact-finding, briefly share with the group what you discovered. Pray for those discussed and set a later time to get together and make plans to meet any urgent needs.

Reasons for Neglecting the Chronically Ill

Last week we raised the question, "Why are we not more concerned about the chronically ill?" Here are some answers to the problem.

1 *We use ourselves as a measuring stick.* Even though we don't mean to be, women can be very judgmental. Often we do not realize that is what we are doing. It is a normal reaction to want to compare a personal experience. If a friend is in a storm that we have survived, we want to share our personal experiences with her. In an attempt to help her, we often begin our discussion with, "Well, when I . . ." We know that the circumstances are not the same, even if the events are similar, and yet we cannot help but compare the two scenarios.

For example, no two breast cancer stories will ever be the same. Just because it did not emotionally devastate me and I was able to work through most of my treatments does not mean that another person should be able to do the same. If you have "been there, done that," clearly you do have more insight into the process, but please be very careful not to assume that you know what the other person is going through.

- If you use your experience to give insight and compassion to the situation, you have done well.

- If you use your experience as a tool to set goals and/or a timeline for someone else, you have actually judged.

Even though our intentions might be to help, the act of running someone else's life based on our experience is judgmental behavior. So, if in doubt, err on the side of compassion. Remember the words of Jesus:

> For with what judgment you judge, you will be judged;
> and with the measure you use, it will be measured back
> to you (Matthew 7:2).

Isn't that a sobering thought?

* Do you find that you are more compassionate or less compassionate to those who are struggling with problems that you have faced? Why?

_____

_____

_____

* Do you believe if you overcame something difficult, everyone else should be able to overcome that problem as well? Why or why not?

_____

_____

Why has the way of the wicked prospered? Why are all those who deal in treachery at ease?
— Jeremiah 12:1 (NASB)

② *We want to know why.* Some people are "observers" and others are "fixers." When a fixer sees a problem, she feels driven to meet the immediate need—fix it and prevent it from reoccurring. In order to do that, the fixer has to understand why the problem occurred in the first place. So fixers have a tendency to jump in and start with corrections, such as:

- "Are you sick because you are not eating well, have bad health habits, or are not receiving proper care?"

- "Is it possible to help you make changes that will improve your health and prevent you from suffering or being in crisis in the future?"

While this fix-it attitude can be very helpful and sometimes answers can be found, that is not always the case.

Haven't we known ladies with a "life event" that began a domino effect that caused every part of their lives to spiral out of control? Their physical bodies were sick, their houses were a mess, their finances were in shambles, their children were out of control, and their marriages were on the brink of disaster. Maybe at one time their lives looked just like yours. There were good days and bad days, but life was manageable. But once "the event" happened, the bad days were overwhelming and the good days were few and far between. It was no longer about managing life but simply surviving.

Of course we also know individuals who have never had manageable lives. Maybe they grew up in dysfunctional homes or have made poor decisions and struggled in every way imaginable. These folks can also find themselves with long-term needs.

Consider this truth: *It is not our duty to know why.* God knows. Often when a person has long-term needs, we want to blame someone or something. That is normal. Note Jesus' answer to the following "why" question.

> And His disciples asked Him, saying, "Rabbi, who sinned, this man or his parents, that he was born blind?" Jesus answered, "It was neither that this man sinned, nor his parents; but it was in order that the works of God might be displayed in him" (John 9:2–3).

❀ Is there a circumstance where understanding "why" would better enable you to help the suffering? How so?

_____

_____

_____

❀ Do you find it easier to help some more than others, depending on the cause of the situation? Why or why not?

_____

_____

_____

❀ Are there some situations where help should not be offered? Why or why not?

_____

_____

_____

> *Do not fear any of those things which you are about to suffer.*
> —Revelation 2:10

❸ *We become overwhelmed at not only the amount of help needed, but also the long-term needs of the situation.* There is not one woman reading this lesson today who enjoys a perfect life. We all have struggles, bills, illnesses, and challenges. Life is hard. Let's face it, ladies. Even the church is not exempt from the fact that ten percent of the people do ninety percent of the work.

I know that's right! If those other people would help us, it wouldn't be as hard on anyone. So how do we get them off the couch! —Sister Sidekick

Reasons for Neglecting, Repeated

We've learned a lot from the three points just studied. Let's repeat them here, and resolve to face the challenges presented.

1 *We use ourselves as a measuring stick.*

2 *We want to know why.*

3 *We become overwhelmed at not only the amount of help needed but also the long-term needs of the situation.*

Don't Go Away

If you are in this Bible study, you are to be commended. You care. You are trying. I suspect that you are part of that working ten percent. As such, you are tired. You're trying to juggle your needs, the needs of your family, and other good works, while simultaneously helping the less fortunate. When this happens I always get the mental image of a mother lion growling and nipping at the cubs crawling all over her. To those watching, the babies appear cute as they nurse, playfully bite her, pull at her ears, and walk all over her resting body. She will tolerate this for a long time, but eventually she reaches her limit. One moment the scene is peaceful and quiet and the next she roars and puts her teeth on the offending cub. The lesson here is that even the strongest of women reach their breaking point.

We can do only so much. Sometimes when we try to do it all, we become overwhelmed and lash out. It's a normal reaction, although it can be a very destructive one.

❋ What are the signs that you have taken on too much and are near-
ing your breaking point?

Stress, not interest no more.

❋ Do the legitimate needs of the sufferer change just because we have
become overwhelmed? Why or why not?

no

❋ How do you feel when you realize you have "lost it" and nipped
at the innocent?

❋ Name some simple things you can do to bless others that could be
done on a long-term basis and *not* become overwhelming to you.

  *Then Jesus said to the twelve, "Do you also want to
go away?" But Simon Peter answered Him, "Lord, to
whom shall we go? You have the words of eternal life."*
—John 6:67–68

Acceptance and Complacency

We all enjoy helping someone with a short-term need. When a
crisis is new, emotions run high, sympathy is overflowing, and
folks line up to do what they can to make things better. However,
as the weeks, months, and years ebb away, so does the support.

This lessening interest is not a negative reflection on our love, compassion, or even our Christianity. It is simply this: *Their abnormal has become normal.* We come to accept the illness, absence, intense suffering, and constant needs as normal, so we become less attentive to the problem.

Our ability to accept things we cannot change is God-given. It enables us to survive. That can be a good thing, but often complacency comes with acceptance. And complacency is the true root of the lack of service to the long-term needy. It's not wrong to accept the fact that life has changed, but when we stop trying to improve the conditions and give comfort to the suffering, a bad situation can become much worse for the victims and their families.

Battling Loneliness and Instability

Long-term suffering can be especially lonely. On good days a sister may be able to do some of the things that she used to be able to do. She may have days or even weeks in which she feels good and rejoins life at least on a small scale.

Eventually though, the disease will rear its ugly head and the victim will be sick again, not only battling the physical pain her illness brings but also the emotional pain that comes along with that kind of yo-yo life.

Sadly, some of us might add to their burden because we do not understand their on-again off-again participation and attendance. In fact, we may go as far as to compare their situation to our own, state what we believe is the cause of the problem, and even nip at the victim. When that happens, it may sound something like this:

Oh, let me do it! They would say something like, "Well, I saw her at the movies last night. If she is well enough to go to the movies, she should be well enough to come to church." —Sister Sidekick

We might even add, "When I am sick I stay at home on Saturday night just to make sure I can go to church on Sunday morning. After all, church is much more important than a movie!"

Without knowing the full story, we have just tried and convicted our sister.

- Maybe that movie was the first time she was able to leave the house in weeks.

- Maybe the mornings are horrible and she feels better at night.

- Maybe her condition is so unpredictable that staying home on Saturday night would have had no bearing on what happened Sunday morning.

- Maybe she is not there because her husband got sick and she stayed home to care for him.

- Maybe she was in an auto accident on the way home.

How Do I Know? The Bible Tells Me So.

God has not called us to be judge and jury. We are called to minister to the suffering in *His* name. So how do we care for the long-term sufferers?

For whoever gives you a cup of water to drink in My name, because you belong to Christ, assuredly, I say to you, he will by no means lose his reward.

—Mark 9:41

Last week, we learned from the Bible example of blind Bartimaeus. This week, we will learn from another sufferer in Mark 2:1–12. Turn there now and read.

We see a man even more disabled than Bartimaeus. He was paralyzed, unable to walk, and totally dependent on others. The obstacles that stood between him and Jesus were much greater. There was a great crowd to get through and great physical exertion was needed. Jesus healed both sufferers, but remember, we are not looking at Jesus or the sick. We are looking at those with them.

Then they came to Him, bringing a paralytic who was carried by four men.

—Mark 2:3

In the example of blind Bartimaeus, those nearby were actually a part of the problem, not the solution. Not only did they *not* help, but they also added to the suffering of the blind man by trying to prevent him from getting to Jesus. We, of course, want to be in the good part of the paralytic's story.

Applying the "Friend" Example

How can we learn from the example of Bartimaeus's friends?

1. Work as a team.

2. Think outside the box to get the job done.

3. Do not be discouraged by the crowd.

❶ *Work as a team.* Did you notice they worked in a group? Caring for the chronically ill is a very emotionally and physically draining job. During my illness, I watched as those around me gave way to the stresses that my illness caused. The pattern was very predictable.

First, they all started off with great enthusiasm, energy, and love. Nothing I asked was too much; they had time to spare to help me. But as time went on, both the physical and emotional demands of my situation began to drain them.

Next, they began to look for ways to "fix things." After all, if I had "no needs," they could walk away without guilt. Sometimes that strategy was helpful, but there were some issues that just could not be fixed.

Finally, the stresses of the situation would get to one of us, and we would "snap" just like that mother lion. There followed a cooling-off period, which gave everyone a much-needed break, but not without both parties involved walking away feeling very wounded.

I found this pattern to be true with loved ones, church members, and even physicians. The ability to stay in an impossible situation should not be used as a measuring stick for love or commitment. Often, the deeper the love we have for someone, the more difficult it is for us to watch them suffer.

This explains why our closest loved ones are often the first to collapse under the stress of chronic illness. Most people do not understand this concept, so instead of sympathy and support, that loved one is judged and chastised because of a seeming lack of care. I've heard it said, "But you're her sister, so you should be able to do this." Of course that is not true. Sometimes we forget that those of the support group are suffering too. That misunderstanding of actions and motives only adds to the suffering of everyone involved.

Working as a team is the best way to avoid burnout for everyone. With teamwork, you can give each other a break, uplift one another, and support and minister to the one who is ill.

❷ *Think outside the box to get the job done.* I seriously doubt that the men who carried their friend to Jesus were planning to remove the roof before they arrived, but once there, it was clear that achieving their goal would require more than just dropping him off.

> And when they could not come near Him because of the crowd, they uncovered the roof where He was. So when they had broken through, they let down the bed on which the paralytic was lying (Mark 2:4).

We sometimes have a predisposed idea of what caring for the sick looks like. If cards, calls, gifts, or food don't cover it, we aren't sure what to do. By using the team approach discussed above, a couple of people with great organizational skills could visit the person, assess the needs of the situation, and the group can decide the best course of action to minister efficiently to the needs of the one who is ill.

It may be that the suffering person needs help with her taxes, research and applications for government programs, information on new medical procedures, or just paying bills and keeping the checkbook balanced. Maybe she needs home repairs or home modifications, such as ramps and lifts. She may require rides to appointments or repairs for her own vehicle. She might appreciate having her home cleaned once a month or her grass mowed. The list is endless.

Just a few minutes spent truly listening to the needy might open a world of possibilities. Once the list of needs and resources has been gathered, the work load can be spread over several groups, so the load is not too much for any one person. We are a family. If everyone does a little, it should not be too much on any one person. Of course, soliciting the help of those who do not normally participate is key. I think you may be pleasantly surprised. Most people are willing to do things in their comfort zone. So "zone them."

Research! I can do that. That would be fun.

—Sister Sidekick

❸ *Do not be discouraged by the crowd.* Both the blind man and the paralytic encountered the obstacle of the crowd in getting to Jesus. In our first story, those in the crowd attempted to hush Bartimaeus. In the second story, the crowd was simply an obstacle that needed to be overcome. Either way, the crowd was a part of the problem, not the solution.

Sometimes well-meaning Christians will either try to silence you or simply stand in the way. That's all right. When we know better, we do better. You can teach them. Remember, discouragement is Satan's tool, not God's.

The key to overcoming discouragement lies in allowing those who are tired to rest with no guilt. Understanding the signs of burnout and stepping back before that happens will allow your teams to be successful. Set up a rotating system. Volunteer workers are more likely to endure tough times if they know what is expected of them and for how long.

But I always feel guilty when I take a break! Well, maybe I wouldn't if it wasn't "my turn."

—Sister Sidekick

Look in your survival kit and hold your flashlight. As you consider the facts and emotion of chronic illness, remind yourself of Christ's light and the love He has for the world. Jot in your journal how you can show that light to the hurting.

"SIDE-BY-SIDE" SURVIVAL KIT

Research Completion

Preparation and planning are key to a successful ministering program. Next week I pray that your group will begin to create your own system that will work well in your home church. Please come prepared next week to do just that.

1 Bring all the info on your sick and shut-in, along with your great ideas and attitudes.

2 Please remember to pray. If God is not in the program it will surely fail.

As you go about your week, please consider these questions carefully:

- Am I someone who rebukes the suffering, telling them not to bother Jesus?
- Am I willing to do whatever it takes, including tearing the roof off of a house, to get help for my brothers and sisters in Christ?

If you do not like the answers to those questions, you have time to pray that God will change your heart. Then you can come back next week willing to become someone you have never been before. The Christian walk is about growing and changing to be more like Jesus. Look back at both stories and ask yourself, "What would Jesus do?" When you get the answer, do that!

What If the Sky Should Fall?

*I clothe the heavens with blackness, and I
make sackcloth their covering.*

—Isaiah 50:3

♪♪ Song ♫

Blessed Assurance

Pledge

I do hereby pledge to begin each Bible study with prayer.

I will ask God to open my heart to the suffering and struggles of others, to give me courage to admit my own faults, to ask for help, and to keep anything I hear during these classes in the strictest of confidence.

I pledge not only to give advice but also to take it.

I pledge to seek out the counsel of an older person and to give respect to those women who have walked the path before me.

I pledge to do all of these things humbly and in a manner that gives glory to God.

Whew! This is an intense study. Thank you for hanging with me. Perhaps you are thinking, "I hope she's almost through beating us up." Trust me, that is not my intent. However, most of us fail at this type of ministry. It's tough. Caring for our long-term sick or disabled members can be a most difficult job in our Christian walk, but it can also be one of the most rewarding. The key is creating a system that works for those needing the help and those giving it. The first and most important step is realizing the need.

Step Up and Help

We must get real and admit that there are those among us who have been forgotten. Sadly, many will just stop asking. It's embarrassing, frustrating, and extremely humbling to admit that you cannot meet even the most basic of your own needs. Trust me, these people did not choose to live a life of suffering and helplessness! I've been there.

Having to ask for help creates feelings of depression, fear, and often anger. No one wants to feel they are a burden. Being forced into a position in which you constantly need help and have little to offer in return is a place that no one chooses, especially the strong willed and very independent.

Don't forget that many of these people were generous givers, and now they must receive. It is not a comfortable predicament. Regardless of the reason they need help, let's not make their situation worse with our complacency. The truth is, they need our help. Some may take it readily, others may need to be persuaded, but God holds each of us accountable for caring for those less fortunate. When abnormal becomes normal, we must all step up and help.

Please use today's lesson as a catalyst to begin something wonderful in your local church.

❋ Take out a pen and paper. As a group, name everyone in your congregation who is chronically ill or disabled.

- Beside each name, write their needs. (Be specific.)
- Check the list carefully and supply the names of any who have been omitted.

❋ What resources can the local church offer to the suffering? For example, mechanics, house cleaners, accountants, medical personnel, computer technicians, transportation providers, sitters, etc.

_____

_____

_____

❋ How can those in need be made aware of the resources your church has available?

_____

_____

❋ What community or government-based programs are available in your area that will help your long-term needy?

_____

_____

❋ What churches or civic organizations in your area can provide you with ideas or information?

_____

_____

❋ How much time has your group spent in prayer over these issues?

_____

❋ What needs cannot be met by your congregation?

_____

_____

🌸 What is the most compassionate way to communicate what your group can and cannot do for the suffering?

Know Better, Do Better

An ancient missionary once said, "Being unwanted, unloved, uncared for, forgotten by everybody, I think that is a much greater hunger, a much greater poverty than the person who has nothing to eat."

This lesson is meant to open your eyes and prick your heart. It is not meant to condemn or scold. The ones studying this lesson are probably already doing the work. The goal here is to become better organized and to involve those who are not active in service.

Our men and our children are wonderful resources we seldom overuse. Give them a chance to serve. The blessings that come from this type of work can be shared by all. Emotions work well short term, but the needs of our chronically ill or disabled are best met with a well-thought-out planned approach.

Look for signs of burnout, take turns, and make sure those receiving help feel loved and appreciated. Don't feel you must meet all the needs of all the people all the time. One glass of cold water given with the right attitude does more good than a whole meal served as a duty. Remember, these people are sick, disabled, or old; not stupid.

My prayer is that today's lesson is just the beginning. If you walk away feeling unworthy, shake your head and cry, but take no action, I have failed. If you leave with a better understanding of the problem and the beginnings of a plan to correct and serve, I have done what I believe God sent me to do.

The truth is, when we know better, we do better. So my question for you is a simple one. You see the problem and have discussed some solutions, so . . . now, what are you going to do?

Journal Notes from a Suffering Christian

I developed this lesson with the help of a wonderful Christian woman who is now deceased. Peggy Walker created a personal journal for each of us to consider. Please take the time to give each question from her journal careful and honest consideration. It is only when we look deep within ourselves that we can be moved to make the changes that God requires. I was both humbled and moved by the questions. I believe you will be too.

My Personal Journal

❋ How do I really feel about the chronically ill? Am I overwhelmed? Afraid it might someday be me? Do I find them difficult to be around?

❋ What things in my comfort zone could I do to help?

* If I am chronically ill, will I allow myself to feel less of a Christian woman because I can no longer serve as I once did? Have I accepted the fact that allowing others to serve me is also allowing God to use me in His mighty plan?

  _____

  _____

* Even though I battle chronic illness, is there anything I can do to serve others?

  _____

  _____

  _____

My Prayer for My Journal

Regardless of where you find yourself in this topic, God can help you. Look deep within your heart and ask Him for what you need. Do not be afraid to get real with God. Remember, He made you, He knows you, and He loves you. Ask and you shall receive.

If desired, use your personal journal in your Side-by-Side Survival Kit to continue the prayer below with your personal sentiments:

Dear Lord and merciful Father, I come to You now asking for Your help. I know I am weak and You are strong. Please God, I need You. Please help me

_____

_____

PART 3

Lions, Tigers, and Bears—Oh My!

FEAR, DEPRESSION, AND OTHER NORMAL EMOTIONS

Side by Side through Thick or Thin
Martha and Gladys

Martha became my friend in college, and we have been close since that time. We have always been a listening and confidential ear for each other. We survived getting married one week apart, our children growing up, and now we're in the retirement years, which require a lot of side-by-side support! Martha has survived a triple bout with cancer, and I persevered through open-heart valve replacement surgery. Believe me, we can both relate to the question, "What if the sky should fall?"

But as the song says, "As long as we're together, it doesn't matter at all." I am thankful for her every day. Praying, laughing, or crying, we have been quite a team. We know we will be there for each other through thick or thin. Side by side until the end, Martha and Gladys, friends for life! To make it even better, our husbands are also friends. Maybe not quite as close as the two of us, yet good friends.

—Gladys Branch, Alabama

WEEK SEVEN

The Same as We Started—Strong!

The righteous cry out, and the Lord hears, and delivers them out of all their troubles. The Lord is near to those who have a broken heart, and saves such as have a contrite spirit. Many are the afflictions of the righteous, but the Lord delivers him out of them all.

—Psalm 34:17–19

♪♪ Song ♬

Just a Closer Walk with Thee

Pledge

I do hereby pledge to begin each Bible study with prayer.

I will ask God to open my heart to the suffering and struggles of others, to give me courage to admit my own faults, to ask for help, and to keep anything I hear during these classes in the strictest of confidence.

I pledge not only to give advice but also to take it.

I pledge to seek out the counsel of an older person and to give respect to those women who have walked the path before me.

I pledge to do all of these things humbly and in a manner that gives glory to God.

The Brave Woman

My husband was at home sick that day in October 1999. In the afternoon we watched a popular daytime talk show together. Since October was breast cancer awareness month, the show host introduced the world to an amazingly brave woman who was battling breast cancer. I don't remember her name, but her story still lives in my heart.

After a long hard fight, it was obvious the woman with cancer was not going to live. Instead of just waiting for the end to come, she did something remarkable. She made videotapes to leave behind for her young daughter. In her recordings, she covered practically everything imaginable—make-up, dating, and wedding-day advice, as well as her blessing for her husband, the girl's father, to remarry. I was in awe of her bravery and her lack of fear of death. It was extremely powerful.

Both Greg and I were touched by the woman's story. After the show, we discussed the tragedy of being diagnosed at such a young age with young children at home. Our hearts bled for that family about to lose a dearly loved wife and mother.

That Woman Could Be Me

That night, as I climbed into the shower, my heart still ached for the stricken family. Just to be sure, I decided to do a breast self-exam. I was shocked to find that the whole top of my left breast was as hard as a rock! This was not a small lump or hard pea under the skin. It was not the size of a raisin or blueberry or even a raspberry, like they had shown on the commercials. My mass was the size of the palm of my hand! I went downstairs and showed my husband. And we both knew I was in trouble.

A needle core biopsy confirmed our greatest fear. I had breast cancer: stage 2 ductal carcinoma to be exact. I was terrified! I was forty-three years old with two middle school children, one high school child, a new job, and a new house. I was living in a new area hundreds of miles from family, wondering, "How will this end? Do I need to start making tapes to leave my children?" I was afraid—deeply afraid!

Reactions and Reality

My breast cancer diagnosis wasn't in my plan. No real family history, a recent clear mammogram, breast fed all three of my children, no risk factors; this was not supposed to happen to me.

Looking back, the whole experience was most humbling. As my family and friends heard the news, the reactions were as different as their owners. For some, the fear was so palpable it was difficult to look them in the face. Others were so upbeat and positive, I wondered if they truly understood my situation. Some gave hugs, cards, and flowers while others tried to make jokes. I was bombarded with stories of friends or loved ones who had experienced different types of cancer and lived. Of course, my favorite was when someone launched into a story, only to get halfway through and realize that the person they were telling me about had died.

They all handled it their own way. That is how it should be. As for me, I became a great actress. At work I smiled, did my job, and wore a wig so as to not frighten the children at school. At home, I was more myself, but the shower was where I would let my hair down (even when I had none) and cry. Alone as the water rushed over my weak body, I wondered, "Is this my last Thanksgiving, Christmas, or New Year? Am I going to die?"

Was I wrong to be afraid? Was I wrong to cry? Is it a lack of faith or displeasing to God when we feel fear? Did you know that the concept of the phrase "Do not be afraid" is recorded over sixty-five times in scripture?

But the very hairs of your head are all numbered. Do not fear therefore; you are of more value than many sparrows.

—Luke 12:7

Hey! I'm not afraid of anything! Well, except spiders or needles or my bathroom scales or . . .

—Sister Sidekick

Negative Emotions

Sadly, I have been told by some well-meaning sisters that fear is a sign of weakness or lack of faith. Prolonged fear can cause depression. Is depression a lack of faith? What about frustration, anger, disappointment, loneliness, or sadness? Are these negative emotions all displeasing to God? Are we, as Christian women, called to live a life in which we are never allowed to have a bad day? Of course not. Jesus was perfect and His life was filled with emotions, both negative and positive. Jesus cried, became angry, and was so emotional in the garden that "His sweat was like drops of blood falling to the ground" (Luke 22:44).

So what do we do with those negative emotions? Do the scriptures shed any light on how to handle the valleys in our lives? Let's look at one man who understood what it was like to be both afraid and depressed. What did God do to help our friend? God the Father came to his rescue.

Elijah: Begin with the End in Mind

First Kings 17 is where we first meet Elijah, a great prophet of God who was the spiritual conscience of God's people during the time of the divided kingdom. We'll begin the examination of his character by taking a fast-forward look at the end of his life.

❋ Read 2 Kings 2:11. How did Elijah leave the earth?

_____

❋ Years later Elijah would be seen again. Read Mark 9:2–13 and explain in your own words what has just happened and why it is important.

_____

_____

_____

_____

Clearly, Elijah was someone special. He was a prophet who left the earth in a miraculous way, reappeared with Jesus, and was one of the most respected leaders of the Israelites, right up there with Moses and Abraham. Surely someone that close to God and His promises could get through life with no problems, right?

God Supplies Needs

Let's go back to the beginning of Elijah's story. In 1 Kings 17, Elijah is sent to King Ahab to inform him that there would be neither dew nor rain for years until Elijah said so. This is a death sentence for the people. No rain meant no food.

Was God being cruel? No, He was punishing Ahab for his wickedness and disciplining the people for following after false gods.

And Ahab made a wooden image. Ahab did more to provoke the Lord God of Israel to anger than all the kings of Israel who were before him (1 Kings 16:33).

God took care of Elijah during those difficult days by sending him to a ravine where he drank from a brook and was fed both meat and bread by ravens (1 Kings 17:2–7). Pretty cool, huh? As the drought became worse, the brook dried up and God sent Elijah to Zarephath of Sidon to be fed and cared for by a widow and her son.

During those years, Elijah was possibly aware that people around him slowly died from starvation and thirst. Most of us have never seen that kind of suffering. But God kept Elijah, the widow, and her son alive with a miraculous supply of oil and flour.

> For thus says the Lord God of Israel: "The bin of flour shall not be used up, nor shall the jar of oil run dry, until the day the Lord sends rain on the earth" (1 Kings 17:14).

Describe what you believe Elijah saw and heard every day as he waited for God to send word that the drought was finally over. What does a country that is suffering from starvation and thirst really look like?

That's just too hard! I don't want to think about it! —Sister Sidekick

Stop the Drought!

When I think of that time, I picture small children's ribs showing with distended bellies and gaunt eyes, old folks too weak to move, mothers with crying babies because their breasts would produce no milk, and the sounds of the suffering and the smell of death everywhere. Daily there would be screams from grieving loved ones as the suffering finally ended with the death of their loved one.

No, the widow was not being melodramatic when she told Elijah that she was collecting sticks so she could prepare the last meal for her and her son. That was the harsh reality of a drought in that part of the country. Yes, God saved Elijah's life, but the years were not easy. Even the widow's son died and a distraught Elijah cried out to the Lord, pleading for the restoration of his life. God answered Elijah's prayer and returned the son to his mother, but most mothers were not that blessed (1 Kings 17:17–23).

After three long years, it was finally time to return to Ahab and stop the drought. Sometimes we read of extreme times and events like that without ever giving them a second thought. What if you were sentenced to prison for three years? Would that seem like a long time? Elijah was caught up in a type of prison. He was trapped there until God told him it was time to leave. For three years, Elijah waited for word from God that the drought was over. Finally, it was time.

> *"Now therefore, send and gather all Israel to me on Mount Carmel, the four hundred and fifty prophets of Baal, and the four hundred prophets of Asherah, who eat at Jezebel's table."*
>
> —1 Kings 18:19

Summon the False Prophets

Elijah made his way to Samaria, and on his way he met Ahab's servant Obadiah, a devoted believer in God. In fact, while Jezebel was killing the prophets of God, Obadiah hid a hundred prophets in two caves and provided food and water to keep them alive.

Obadiah was thrilled to see Elijah but warned him his life was in danger and told him about the hidden prophets (1 Kings 18:7–13).

Imagine how Obadiah felt when Elijah said, "Tell Ahab I'm here." Obadiah was reluctant but he followed instructions. Unafraid, Elijah appeared to King Ahab and instructed him to summon all of Israel along with the 450 prophets of Baal and the 400 prophets of Asherah to Mt. Carmel.

Pause right now and read about this event (1 Kings 18:20–46). I could never do it justice trying to condense it., but here is a small portion of it.

"Hear me, O Lord, hear me, that this people may know that You are the Lord God, and that You have turned their hearts back to You again." Then the fire of the Lord fell and consumed the burnt sacrifice, and the wood and the stones and the dust, and it licked up the water that was in the trench. Now when all the people saw it, they fell on their faces; and they said, "The Lord, He is God! The Lord, He is God!"

—1 Kings 18:37–39

Power-Packed Event

We love that dramatic story. Can't you visualize those prophets of Baal dancing, cutting themselves, and crying out for hours while Elijah mocked them openly. Then when it was Elijah's turn, he was so confident that he made it harder to burn his offering, and yet God demonstrated His power for all to see. Awesome!

The squeamish side of me is not so excited about the gruesome scene that came next. Elijah ordered that all 450 prophets of Baal be captured and killed. God needed to eradicate the evil from His land, and killing the prophets was a necessary part of that cleansing. What a victory!

Then we see Elijah confidently telling the king that the rain was coming (1 Kings 18:41). A bold, triumphant, powerful, excited Elijah prayed on the mountain and seven times sent his servant to look for rain. Seven times! Not once, not twice, but seven times Elijah sent the servant, knowing that God would fulfill His promise. Then of course, the cloud was there and Elijah actually outran the king's chariot. What bravery! What faith! What boldness! What strength! Elijah was a great prophet of God. Elijah was amazing.

Stay Tuned for the Storm to Hit after the Rain

Elijah is one of those prophets we love to love, but his story is not just one of victory. Serving God in a mighty way is not an easy way of life.

In the following lesson, we will look at the next chapter of Elijah's life that is not so victorious. If you know it, don't give it away. If you don't know it, then brace yourself and remember: Elijah was human, just like you and me. Isn't it wonderful that God's word allows us to see not only the victories of the spiritual leaders of the past, but their struggles as well? In this chapter, we are rejoicing in Elijah's triumph over adversity. Next week we will look more closely at his struggles and how God ministered to Elijah during difficult days.

Use the questions below to begin a conversation about life's ups and downs. Do not limit yourself to these questions. Share your thoughts. No one has all the answers. As I have said many times, "I don't have all the answers, I just want to get the conversation started."

❋ I shared my breast cancer experience. Please share a time in your life when you were truly afraid.

✸ Do you believe fear is a sign of spiritual weakness? Why or why not?

_____

_____

✸ Why do you believe that some of us are more afraid than others given the same set of circumstances?

_____

_____

Don't Know What's Coming Tomorrow

Jezebel sent a messenger to Elijah, saying, "So let the gods do to me, and more also, if I do not make your life as the life of one of them by tomorrow about this time." And when he saw that, he arose and ran for his life . . . he himself went a day's journey into the wilderness, and came and sat down under a broom tree, and he prayed that he might die.

—1 Kings 19:2–4

 Song

God Will Take Care of You (Be Not Dismayed)

Pledge

I do hereby pledge to begin each Bible study with prayer.

I will ask God to open my heart to the suffering and struggles of others, to give me courage to admit my own faults, to ask for help, and to keep anything I hear during these classes in the strictest of confidence.

I pledge not only to give advice but also to take it.

I pledge to seek out the counsel of an older person and to give respect to those women who have walked the path before me.

I pledge to do all of these things humbly and in a manner that gives glory to God.

We are continuing our examination of Elijah to help us get real about fear, depression, and other normal emotions. So far in our story Elijah has shown great strength, faith, and endurance. He has even given us a reason to chuckle as he mocked the false prophets desperate to get an answer from their fake god (1 Kings 18).

If I were writing a book about Elijah's experience, I would stop the story right there. That book would be a New York Times best seller, closely followed by a movie that is a box office hit—an epic film with extreme highs and lows. The audience would cry as people die from starvation, laugh as Elijah mocks the false prophets, cheer as fire comes down and consumes the altar, and be inspired by a thin, dirty, worn-looking prophet who lifts his voice to God in prayer.

I can see it now. The last scene is Elijah, wind in his hair, dust flying under his sandals, running with all his might as raindrops fall from above. The sky is dark, lightening is flashing, drums are booming, and trumpets are blaring the sounds of victory. Then the camera pulls back exposing a man in a chariot wildly beating his horse to keep up with the runner, but the distance between the two only increases as our hero races his way back to the city.

Oh yes, if I were writing the story, that is where I would stop. Any crowd would be uplifted as they leave the theater, once again reassured that the good guy always wins. The ending, although predictable, would be enough to keep them on an emotional high for days to come.

But I did not write this story. Men inspired by God wrote the story and thankfully for us God did not stop there.

Afraid!

After years of struggle and hardship, Elijah had an enormous victory. He was on top of the world, that is, until he was hit with just one more dark cloud, the proverbial "straw that broke the camel's back." You see, Ahab, the evil king, went home and told the little woman Jezebel what had happened on that mountain.

> Then Jezebel sent a messenger to Elijah, saying, "So let the gods do to me, and more also, if I do not make your life as the life of one of them by tomorrow about this time" (1 Kings 19:2).

So Jezebel was going to take Elijah's life. No big deal, right? Elijah had already stood up to Ahab, knowing that it could cost him his life. He stood toe-to-toe with 850 full-grown men and called down fire from heaven. He ordered the killing of those men, prayed for rain, received it, and outran a chariot, all in one day. Even before that, he had eaten miraculous foods, raised a boy from the dead, and stood face-to-face with one of the most evil kings in Israel's history. He never blinked. A silly threat from a wicked woman was no big deal, right? Or was it?

> And when he saw that, he arose and ran for his life, and went to Beersheba, which belongs to Judah, and left his servant there. But he himself went a day's journey into the wilderness, and came and sat down under a broom tree. And he prayed that he might die, and said, "It is enough! Now Lord, take my life, for I am no better than my fathers!" (1 Kings 19:3–4).

Exhausted!

Really? Seriously? After all he has witnessed? After all the success, bravery, and overcoming? A threat from this woman was causing this great man of God to flee in fear? Yes, as a matter of fact, it was. Why? Look in verse 5. "He lay down under a broom bush and fell asleep."

Elijah was spent. He had endured three extremely difficult years that had left him mentally and physically exhausted. After the battle on the mountain, Elijah probably thought, "Whew, sure glad that's over. I am looking forward to getting back to a normal life again." Of course, having the most evil woman in history threaten your life means that your life will be anything but normal.

✳ Have you been there? Have you ever had a difficult time in your life you thought would never end? How did you get through it? How did you feel when it was finally over?

_____

_____

_____

✳ How can victory stress body and soul as much as defeat?

_____

_____

We all love a happy ending. We struggle with the hero through the tale just to get to "and they lived happily ever after." We leave Cinderella marrying the prince, Snow White awakened by a kiss, and little Red Riding Hood being rescued. The good guys always win. The fancily scripted phrase *The End* flashes on the screen, and we walk away wearing smiles.

Swap the Fairy Tale for a Survival Kit

Of course, that is how it happens in fairy tales. In real life the dramatic victories are often followed by yet another challenge which might be the one that defeats you. You've fought, you're tired, you're ready for life to get back to normal, and boom. Then you get hit with one more issue. One more fight. One more challenge. When that happens, you are your weakest. Exhausted from the past, you cannot begin to picture getting up and fighting another time. I believe that is why this great prophet of God ran in fear.

So what did God the Father do for His weary prophet? What can we learn from His example when it comes to dealing with fear, depression, and frustration? Pay attention and record God's actions in your journal.

❶ *Eat something.* "Then as he lay and slept under a broom tree, suddenly an angel touched him, and said to him, 'Arise and eat.' Then he looked, and there by his head was a cake baked on coals, and a jar of water. So he ate and drank, and lay down again. And the angel of the Lord came back the second time, and touched him, and said, 'Arise and eat, because the journey is too great for you'" (1 Kings 19:5–7).

✺ Who did God send to help Elijah?

_____

✺ What is the value of touch when one is exhausted?

_____

✺ What physical needs did God meet by doing this?

_____

_____

Elijah is mentally and physically exhausted and afraid for his life. God knows that. He saw all the problems Elijah had been through. First, God met Elijah's physical needs: rest, food, and safety.

When we or our loved ones are going through difficult times, we must follow God's example. First, take care of the physical needs. God did not lecture Elijah, remind him of the battle he had just won, or give him a pep talk. He first allowed Elijah to rest and eat. Notice that Elijah's provisions were simple. God did not zap him to a five-star hotel and a seven-course meal. He met Elijah's basic needs, and that was enough.

What did God do next?

❷ *Get up again but take time to ponder.* "So he arose, and ate and drank; and he went in the strength of that food forty days and forty nights as far as Horeb, the mountain of God" (1 Kings 19:8).

> ✱ Where did Elijah go and what was the miracle associated with this journey?

_____

God gave him time. For forty days Elijah made his way to Mount Horeb, almost certainly on foot. He needed time to reflect, absorb, and think about what had happened over the past few years. God knew that and gave him that time, but don't miss the fact that Elijah was actually walking toward God each day.

After forty days of travel and quiet time to reflect, Elijah reached Mount Horeb. God is the perfect Father and knows what we need. However, having our physical needs met and meditating in quiet time are not always enough.

> And there he went into a cave, and spent the night in that place; and behold, the word of the Lord came to him, and He said to him, "What are you doing here, Elijah?" So he said, "I have been very zealous for the Lord God of hosts; for the children of Israel have forsaken Your covenant, torn down Your altars, and killed Your prophets with the sword. I alone am left; and they seek to take my life" (1 Kings 19:9–10).

> ✱ Has meeting physical needs and time healed Elijah? How do you know that?

_____

_____

❸ *Get with God.* "Then He said, 'Go out, and stand on the mountain before the Lord.' And behold, the Lord passed by and a great and strong wind tore into the mountains and broke the rocks in pieces before the Lord, but the Lord was not in the wind; and after the wind an earthquake, but the Lord was not in the earthquake; and after the earthquake a fire, but the Lord was not in the fire; and after the fire a still small voice. So it was, when Elijah heard it, that he wrapped his face in his mantle and went out and stood in the entrance of the cave. Suddenly a voice came to him, and said, 'What are you doing here, Elijah?' And he said, 'I have been very zealous for the Lord God of hosts; because the children of Israel have forsaken Your covenant, torn down Your altars, and killed Your prophets with the sword. I alone am left; and they seek to take my life'" (1 Kings 19:11–14),

❋ Why do you need the three reminders above for your journal?

_____

_____

 Suddenly a voice came to him, and said, "What are you doing here, Elijah?"

—1 Kings 19:13

Wind, Earthquake, Fire

As a child I remember sermons/lessons on these verses from 1 Kings, and the take away was always the same. That God was not in the big stuff. God was in the little stuff, the "gentle whisper." While I cannot argue with that logic, do you think there might be just a bit more going on here? I believe that God used these three earthly elements to teach Elijah a much more powerful lesson.

Wind

- God started with the wind to remind Elijah of the invisible forces in our lives. Look at the great power of this wind. It literally tore the mountain apart and shattered the rocks. Isn't it amazing that a force we cannot see can do that much damage?

- Our emotions can be such a wind. Fear, anger, depression, frustration, and discouragement cannot be seen by the eye or touched by the hand, but these emotions can tear our world apart. They can tear apart the mountains of trust and relationships that have taken a lifetime to build, and they can shatter the rocks of truth we use to protect and defend ourselves.

- The terrible winds of negative emotions can cause those we love to flee in fear, as insults and anger are hurled with such force as to destroy everything they touch. They can cause us to feel caught up, pushed from side to side, and unable to breathe. We hide our own faces from the storms our emotions create. No, these things cannot be seen, but they have tremendous strength and can do unbelievable damage.

- Was Elijah impressed by such powerful winds? I believe that God was reminding Elijah and us that His power is far greater than our strongest emotional tornadoes.

Earthquake

- God caused an earthquake that shook the very ground where Elijah stood. Most of us have never experienced an earthquake, but we know they are terrifying. Perhaps God shook the earth to remind Elijah about the physical things of this earth. Everything we need—food, clothing, and shelter—comes from the earth. God takes care of our physical needs, and we are told not to worry about such things (Luke 12:27–31).

- God emphasizes that He is there when the ground beneath your feet violently shakes. When you experience a job loss, health crisis, death of a loved one, or loss of earthly possessions, God is there. God did not cause these things to happen. Our lives are controlled by the laws of nature, the free will of man, and Satan's deceiving ways. Yes, God either created or allowed all of those events, but God did not take your job or your loved one from you. God does, however, understand your grief and He will comfort you, bless you, and see you through the earthquake.

Fire

- God has used fire to spiritually connect Him to His people since the beginning of creation. Fire was used for sacrifices, God spoke to Moses from a burning bush, and God used fire to lead the Israelites on their forty-year journey through the wilderness. Elijah called down fire from heaven to reestablish God's power and call the people back to worshiping the one true God. Fire is also mentioned as the key element of hell and the suffering found there (Matthew 5:22; 18:9; Mark 9:43).

- God sent fire as His last message to Elijah, perhaps to remind him of the great power that faith can bring. While the wind can move and break both man and matter, and the earthquake can shake them to their foundations, only fire can literally change the chemical makeup of matter. Fire can turn sand into glass and solid metal into liquid. It can make raw food more palatable and ready for consumption. Fire transforms!

Faith and Destiny

Does God want you to be reminded of the power of faith? Put your faith in God and you will be blessed not only here on earth but for all eternity as well. Put your faith in this earth and its treasures, and your eternal destiny will be the fires of hell. It is faith and spiritual connection to God that can change eternal destiny. If you have enough faith, nothing will be impossible. You can move mountains (Matthew 17:20).

I believe this is one concept we do not fully apply. If we did, nothing or no one could stop us. Great faith equals great power from God. Elijah knew that and so do we, but when the stress of life becomes overwhelming, we need to be reminded of it. God reminded Elijah that the strength born from a true faith in the living God can provide light, power, and strength, and it truly transforms things. Could Elijah hear it?

Where Are You?

Look at the last part of 1 Kings 19:12. "And after the fire a still small voice." What a stark contrast to all the noise, violence, and destruction that Elijah had just witnessed. Where exactly was Elijah when he heard that small voice? Keep reading.

> So it was, when Elijah heard it, that he wrapped his face in his mantle and went out and stood in the entrance of the cave. Suddenly a voice came to him, and said, "What are you doing here, Elijah?" (1 Kings 19:13).

Elijah was in the cave!

I'd be hiding in a cave too! Did you see all that bad stuff that was happening? —Sister Sidekick

God had told Elijah to go and stand on the mountain, and yet when the gentle whisper came, Elijah "went out and stood at the mouth of the cave." Did he never leave the cave? Did he run back to the cave when all the storms raged around him? Did he return to the cave after the magnificent event was over? We don't know. All we are told is that Elijah was in the cave when he heard the still small voice of the Lord and that he went to the mouth of the cave. He did not come out of the cave even when he heard the voice of God. Elijah was depressed.

❋ When the storms of life surround you, where do you go?

There Is More

God loved Elijah. He never left Elijah; He helped him. But up until now, it seems that God's efforts were in vain. After all, Elijah was still in the mouth of the cave. But that is not the end.

Next week we will look at how God met all of Elijah's needs, just as He meets ours. For now, though, the takeaway is this: *God does not forget or abandon us when we are hurting. He cares. He is there. Sometimes we, like Elijah, try to hide from God, but He is waiting outside of our hiding place. It is up to us to emerge.*

God met Elijah's physical needs and gave him time to process what happened to him. There is one more blessing God will give to Elijah and that blessing makes all the difference. In next week's lesson, God writes a doozy of a happy ending.

❋ When someone is mentally and physically exhausted, what is the best way to provide comfort?

There were lots of messages in the wind, rain, and fire God showed Elijah. How might God get our attention when we are in our hiding place?

_____

_____

 Should we hold church leaders to a higher standard than the rest of us when dealing with life's hardships? Why or why not?

_____

_____

_____

Whenever I am afraid, I will trust in You.
—Psalm 56:3

WEEK NINE

As Long as We're Together!

Elisha said, "As the Lord lives, and as your soul lives, I will not leave you!"

—2 Kings 2:2

♪ Song ♫

Bind Us Together

Pledge

I do hereby pledge to begin each Bible study with prayer.

I will ask God to open my heart to the suffering and struggles of others, to give me courage to admit my own faults, to ask for help, and to keep anything I hear during these classes in the strictest of confidence.

I pledge not only to give advice but also to take it.

I pledge to seek out the counsel of an older person and to give respect to those women who have walked the path before me.

I pledge to do all of these things humbly and in a manner that gives glory to God.

We've lived with Elijah the past few weeks to gain insight into fear, depression, and other normal emotions. What have we learned so far? Elijah is one of the best-loved prophets in scripture.

His life teaches us so much about dealing with the ups and downs of our own lives. God loved Elijah and took care of him no matter where he was in his life's journey. When Elijah was at the height of his strength and service to God, God was there. When Elijah was at the depths of despair and fear, God was there. God is the perfect Father who knows how to love and care for His children.

When Elijah was strong, God sent him to do some very important work. Elijah carried out that work with boldness and confidence. But after years of drought and famine, Elijah was both mentally and physical drained. So when Jezebel threatened his life, Elijah crumbled (1 Kings 19). God took care of His servant Elijah. Let's do a quick review of what God did for Elijah.

God met Elijah's _____ needs (1 Kings 19:5–7).
He gave Elijah _strength_ (1 Kings 19:8).
He showed Elijah His power by using _earth_,
wind, and _fire_ (1 Kings 19:11–12).

That should have been enough, right? Roll the sappy music and bring up the fancy *The End*. Elijah is "fully recovered." God blew Elijah away with His power and miracles, and now Elijah is over his fear and depression. I just love a happy ending, don't you? Must be time for another movie.

That's what God did and that's what we should do too, right? When we are depressed or someone we love is struggling, it is just that easy. Meet physical needs, give them time, remind them of God's awesome power, and presto-chango, all is well and they are over all issues. Happy ending. All better now. Done deal. Right? *No, not exactly!*

Seriously? After all that, Elijah is still not getting it? I think God should just wash His hands of that guy! Clearly, Elijah has a real faith problem. —Sister Sidekick

When More Is Needed

Let's get real by getting back to the rest of the story in 1 Kings 19. We left Elijah at the mouth of the cave after God's stupendous miracles. Once again God asks, "What are you doing here, Elijah?" (1 Kings 19:13).

Of course, God knows why Elijah is there. After all, it was God who sent an angel to direct Elijah to Mount Horeb. The question is more about Elijah's emotional state than his physical location.

> And he said, "I have been very zealous for the Lord God of hosts; because the children of Israel have forsaken Your covenant, torn down Your altars, and killed Your prophets with the sword. I alone am left; and they seek to take my life" (1 Kings 19:14).

Elijah's answer, before and after the wind, earthquake, and fire are exactly the same, word for word (1 Kings 19:10, 14). How can that be? How can he see God's great power and talk directly to Him and still be depressed? Still be afraid? Still not want to leave the cave? How can that be?

Elijah was still struggling because he actually needed more. "Blasphemy," some say. "Lack of faith." "A hopeless case." Not so! God knew what Elijah needed, and that's what He gave him.

Exactly what did Elijah need if it wasn't miracles or talking directly to God? Elijah needed someone with skin on. Elijah had a deep faith and respect for God, but he also needed flesh-and-blood people to walk side by side with him and to provide comfort, protection, companionship, and support. How do I know that? Because up to this point, Elijah would not leave the cave, but verse 19 says, "So he departed from there."

Missions with Purpose

Where did Elijah go? He went to accomplish the work that God had given him. Check out 1 Kings 19:15–18.

- Anoint Hazael king over Syria.

- Anoint Jehu king over Israel.

- Anoint Elisha to succeed you as prophet.

Not only did God tell Elijah who to anoint, but He also made a promise to Elijah as to how Hazael, Jehu, and Elisha would protect him. Combining the facts of 1 Kings 19:15–18, 2 Kings 8:7–15, and 2 Kings 9:1–6, we see that Elijah anointed Elisha in person and authorized him to anoint Hazael. Elisha in turn, sent a servant of a prophet to fulfil God's command to anoint Jehu.

> It shall be that whoever escapes the sword of Hazael, Jehu will kill; and whoever escapes the sword of Jehu, Elisha will kill (1 Kings 19:17).

God knew that Elijah was afraid for his life. Did God mock him, rebuke him, and say he had little faith? No. God said, "Go!" God had a mission and a network of support lined up for Elijah. Keep reading.

> Yet I have reserved seven thousand in Israel, all whose knees have not bowed to Baal, and every mouth that has not kissed him (1 Kings 19:18).

Talk about a support system! God provided a full-time companion and seven thousand prophets. It was time for Elijah to move forward. Now he could leave the cave and begin active service to God again.

Don't miss the fact that after Elijah met and anointed Elisha, Elijah went on to serve God mightily, but Elisha was always by his side.

Wow! God really knows how to make you feel protected! —Sister Sidekick

Strength in Troubled Times

When we struggle emotionally, it does not necessarily mean we are weak or lack faith. It might mean that something we need is missing. Some emotional situations may require medication. There is no shame in taking a drug that helps us deal with physical needs. However, for many of us, depression, fear, and frustration are short-term issues and not long-term medical problems. Regardless of the cause, the answers are the same.

❶ *Meet physical needs.* Especially during times of emotional trial, we must eat the proper foods, get plenty of rest, and continue to exercise. If the situation prohibits you from your normal routine, do your best. At the same time, cut yourself some slack. Understand that lack of proper rest and nutrition can make you weaker. Don't set standards for yourself that are unrealistic.

❷ *Meet emotional needs.* Take the time and space to process what is causing the fear and depression. This will vary from person to person and from event to event. There will be times when the same event can bring about two very different reactions. Remember Elijah? His life was threatened more than once, but his reaction to the threat was different each time.

❸ *Meet mental needs.* Lean on God. That is where strength comes from. That is where power is found. Read the scriptures. God's word holds the answers we seek. Pray. Prayer is a powerful tool.

❹ *Pray with your whole being.* Tell God how you are feeling. It is all right to express confusion, fear, disappointment, and even anger over what has happened. Don't forget, God already knows. We are the ones who need to express our feelings to Him. After all, we cannot fully deal with issues that we will not acknowledge.

> *O Lord, You have searched me and known me. You know my sitting down and my rising up; You understand my thought afar off. You comprehend my path and my lying down, and are acquainted with all my ways. For there is not a word on my tongue, but behold, O Lord, You know it altogether.*
>
> —Psalm 139:1–4

✴ Get out your survival kit and review your prayer notes from Week Three "Communication Device" on page 37.

Give God Your Anger

God created the universe and defeated Satan. He can handle your anger. God never said that anger was a sin. We are told not to sin in our anger and not to let the sun go down on our anger; we are *not* told that we cannot be angry (Ephesians 4:26).

Tell God you are angry. Then ask Him to help you deal with not only the situation but also the anger it causes. Ask Him to cause every applicable word of the Holy Spirit to rise up within you and comfort you as never before. Acknowledge that you need His "groanings" with your weaknesses (Romans 8:26). The spiritual blessings we have as Christian women can empower us to endure whatever life throws at us. With God all things truly are possible.

I can do all things through Christ who strengthens me.
—Philippians 4:13

Feelings Don't Deserve Punishment

Many of us suffer in silence because we do not believe we have the right to the feelings that haunt us. We are afraid that if anyone knew how we truly felt, we would be viewed as weak, sinful, or worse—someone who needs to be corrected.

We know that feelings are not facts, but I have never heard of someone overcoming a fear or rising from a depression because she was guilted or chastised out of it. Oh, she might pretend to be better so the sermons will stop, but the pain remains deep within.

If God did not punish Elijah for his fear, who are we to punish others for theirs? Ponder this fact: The one thing Elijah feared most, death, was the one thing that never happened. Don't you love it? Elijah did not die a natural death—He rode to heaven in a chariot! Now that, my sisters, is the act of a loving Father.

Side by Side with the Struggling

To help us realize the actions needed to achieve the status of our chapter title, "As Long as We're Together," ask yourself the following questions:

- Am I the kind of Christian woman who invites others to confide in me during times of distress?
- Do people trust me enough to bare their souls to me?
- Do I understand how to comfort without judging?
- Can I keep secrets?
- Am I willing to walk side by side with a struggling sister in a way that helps her overcome the pain that has overtaken her?
- Can I be an Elisha to my sisters in the Lord?

Remember, Elisha began serving God by serving Elijah as a faithful sidekick during difficult times.

❋ Write the four points you have just studied in your journal under the heading "Strength in Troubled Times." Make any other notes that will help you.

We're Together for the Long Haul

God knew we needed each other. He created us. That's why we are called the family of God. We can worship Him anywhere, anytime, but we must come together to love and support one another. By serving one another, we serve God. Our theme song proclaims,

> *Through all kinds of weather,*
> *What if the sky should fall?*
> *As long as we're together,*
> *It doesn't matter at all.*

Lions, tigers, and bears—oh my! No matter who you are or where you live, you will experience fear, depression, and other negative emotions. Having those emotions is not a sin.

Reach out to your sisters and let them know you are there when they need you. Be bold enough to ask for help when you need it. Let's get real about what it is to be a Christian woman in today's world. It does *not* mean that life will not be problematic. It means when times get tough, you don't have to fight alone.

In *The Wizard of Oz*, Dorothy made her trip with a scarecrow, a tin man, and a cowardly lion. I have a heavenly Father who loves me, the Holy Spirit who provided scriptures to comfort me, and a brother who died for me. However, in those times when I need someone with skin, I have you, my fellow Christian sisters. That makes all the difference!

✽ Was there a time when you, or someone you know, thought the tough times were over, only to be hit with another difficult trial? If so, please share any experience that is not confidential.

✽ Who is your Elisha? What person walks with you no matter how hard life becomes?

✽ What techniques work best when trying to help a struggling sister?

✽ Do you struggle with feeling the need always to be positive and upbeat? What are the pros and cons of doing so?

✽ Of the four needs, physical, mental, spiritual, and emotional, which one is the most difficult to present to a friend for help? How may it comfort us to know that Jesus "grew" in each of these areas and understands our needs?

✹ Does someone in your life need an Elisha? Will you be that Elisha? If not, how can you help find an Elisha for your friend?

_____

_____

_____

✹ Has this lesson made you rethink your feelings about your own emotional struggles? How? Why?

_____

_____

✹ In what ways has this lesson reinforced your resolve to treat others more compassionately in their struggles with their fear, depression, and other normal emotions?

_____

_____

Close your time together in prayer. Ask God for wisdom, humility, and compassion when dealing with your own emotional struggles and the struggles of those around you.

PART 4

The Sin No One Confesses

INVISIBLE FAULTS

Side-by-Side through Stranger Danger
Ann and Dawn

Dawn and I met as freshmen in college and connected immediately. Studious and creative, she taught me to study and kept me from failing. She was a gifted singer, guitarist, and composer, and I was a decent singer. We spent many evenings, singing and harmonizing. We had a lot of fun together—for a while.

As sophomores, we lived in the newest dorm. Cell phones were non-existent, but we had a landline phone in our room. That luxury soon became a source of terror. A man called every night. Sometimes it was heavy breathing. Sometimes, it was vulgar, sexual language. Sometimes there were threats of bodily harm. It had to be someone we knew, but who? Every deep voice was suspicious.

We were not allowed to go anywhere alone. Laws back then dictated that the police could not help us unless the man physically touched us. We had the phone company trace the calls while we kept him talking for 45 minutes. It was horrible listening to his vulgar words.

The offender was arrested and given probation and counseling. Dawn went home at the end of the semester, but I stayed. After his probation ended, the calls began again. My car tires and the seats of my car were slashed. He left a note saying, "You're next!" At one point, he had me at gunpoint in the crowded student center. I screamed, "Fire!" and escaped into the ensuing bedlam. The police told me to get out of town before he killed me. I did.

From a time of terror, to ensuing years of peace, we learned to share our deepest fears—which still surface occasionally. She is the person who listens and sympathizes without jumping to conclusions. And so am I! The Lord is our strength; He brought us through our trials and made us even stronger. We are still "singing a song" treasuring our side-by-side friendship.

— Name Withheld

The Stranger in the Mirror

For if anyone is a hearer of the word and not a doer, he is like a man observing his natural face in a mirror; for he observes himself, goes away, and immediately forgets what kind of man he was.

—James 1:23–24

♪♫ Song ♫

None of Self and All of Thee

Pledge

I do hereby pledge to begin each Bible study with prayer.

I will ask God to open my heart to the suffering and struggles of others, to give me courage to admit my own faults, to ask for help, and to keep anything I hear during these classes in the strictest of confidence.

I pledge not only to give advice but also to take it.

I pledge to seek out the counsel of an older person and to give respect to those women who have walked the path before me.

I pledge to do all of these things humbly and in a manner that gives glory to God.

I think I am losing my mind. It's really a little scary, you know. There's Alzheimer's, menopause, stress, and all kinds of things that I could blame, but it is happening just the same. I seem to be unable to stop it.

I know who I am. I really do. I know my name, what I look like and where I live, and I can actually identify pictures of myself from today all the way back to childhood. Others may have to ask, "Who is that good-looking girl in that old black-and-white photo?" But I know. I've lived with this body, stared at this face, and dealt with this personality for as long as I can remember. I know who I am.

How can it be that in the last few years a stranger is looking back from my mirror? It began slowly at first. A wrinkle, a gray hair, a sag here, a bag there, but I knew how to make it go away. If I stood at a certain angle, created just the right lighting—ah, there I am. That lasted for a few years, but sadly, that body now seems to be disappearing altogether.

I look down and see my mother's hands and feet. My curving spine looks like my dad's, not mine. The reflection in the mirror is no longer me, but a mixture of my parents and grandparents. How did it happen? When did it happen? Why did it happen? I know I am not hallucinating; others see it too.

Recently I went to a family funeral, and more than one person came up to me and said, "You look just like your dad." Really! I look like a man in his eighties? Actually, yes. Yes I do. I look like my dad. However, it is not just dad. There are times when I look in the mirror and see my mother more than myself.

To make matters worse, everyone else already knew it was happening. Is that why I am the only one shocked when I look into the mirror and hardly recognize the face I see? It's just not fair! It was happening to me, so why was I the last to know?

How Do I See Myself?

I have a plan. All mirrors must be removed from my home. I will avoid all plate glass and other reflective surfaces. Photos can be taken, but I will not look at them for at least ten years. (I figure by then I will think I looked pretty good ten years ago.) If I never see my reflection, then it is not happening, right? Then all I will see is *your* concept of me, and I'll say, "Girl, you're lookin' pretty good!"

That's it! She's gone over the edge, and I'm not going after her! —Sister Sidekick

Sigh. I suppose not growing old is not really an option, huh? I guess I will make the best of what I have, wrinkles and all. Or, as we say in kindergarten, "You take what you get and you don't throw a fit."

Has that happened to you? Have you been surprised by what you see in a mirror? Have you caught a glimpse of yourself as you passed by a reflective surface and been caught off guard by your own reflection? Have you seen a photo you knew was you, but didn't recognize the person in the picture?

❋ What is your all-time favorite picture of yourself? Why do you like it so much? Do you feel it actually looks like you or does it make you look better than you believe you really do?

_____

_____

❋ Do you consider yourself attractive? Why or why not?

_____

_____

❋ If you were asked to describe yourself what would you say?

_____

_____

"Do not look at his appearance or at the height of his stature . . . for the Lord does not see as man sees, for man looks at the outward appearance, but the Lord looks at the heart."

—1 Samuel 16:7

The Girl on the Cover

When I was fifteen and a sophomore in high school, I performed in the musical production of *Scrooge*. I also helped with the costumes. One afternoon someone from the local paper came to take some pictures for the cover story. I was chosen to wear one of the costumes and stand in a chair as the others pretended to work on my dress. It was all quite exciting.

However, when the paper arrived I stared at the girl on the cover in disbelief. I knew it had to be me. I was there. Everyone else looked the same, but to this day I will argue that the girl in that photo bore no resemblance to me at all. Maybe it was the lighting or newspaper print or the fact that it was in black and gray shades, but I had no idea who that girl standing in the chair was. It was certainly not me. She was just too pretty.

I have also had the complete opposite experience. I've seen pictures of myself and wondered, "Who is the fat, hunched old lady?" Then at second glance, I'm forced to admit, "It's me." Have you been there? I hear your "Amen."

Oh brother! Here we go again. —Sister Sidekick

The Camera, Unfeeling Machine

As time goes by I slowly become accustomed to my face in the bathroom mirror. Of course, for the most part my mirror shows me only the image I create. I control the lighting, the angle, and the timing. Photos, on the other hand, often show me what everyone else sees. Whether I am pleasantly surprised or alarmingly shocked makes no difference at all to the camera. The camera is not concerned with what I think I look like. It merely produces the image that it sees in that fraction of a second when the lens flicks open. My feelings are *irrelevant.*

 Beauty is but a lease from nature.
—Edward Counsel

What I See Versus the Real Me

Just as there are two views of the physical me, there are two views of the spiritual me as well. There's the me I believe myself to be and the me that others see. I must be willing to look at both views in order to see the whole picture. I know what I see, but what do the people around me see?

- Do they see a woman with a Christian bumper sticker on her car cutting folks off in traffic, breaking the speed limit, and making unkind gestures to anyone who gets her way?

- Do they see a scantily dressed woman decked out in beautifully matching cross necklace and earrings?

- Do they see a woman who spends hours working at the church building while gossiping with everyone who will listen?

- Do they see a woman who attends movies she would not take Christ to see?

- Do they see a woman who reads books she would be embarassed for her Christian family to see on her bookshelf?

I may be in denial of who I really am, but I am not fooling anyone else. What about you? What do others see when they look at you?

- Do they see a woman whose actions match her words?

- Do they see someone who is daily trying to grow spiritually and bring others to Christ?

- Do they see a woman who is in the world, but not of the world?

Pause for a moment and take out your spiritual mirror. Take a good long hard look at yourself. Are you pleased with what you see? Is it possible that for all your trying you cannot see what others see clearly, because you have only one view?

Oh, I'm scared! I may not like what I see!

—Sister Sidekick

 If someone says, "I love God," and hates his brother, he is a liar; for he who does not love his brother whom he has seen, how can he love God whom he has not seen?
—1 John 4:20

Oh, Delilah!

While it is true that others often see clearly what we cannot see ourselves, it is also true that some of us can be masters of disguise. We know that God can see the heart, and we have no secrets from Him. But it *is* possible to fool others, even those closest to us. In fact, love can be blind. I do not recommend asking your spouse or children to point out your faults. They may actually not be able to see them. Insanity you say? Keep reading.

Please! My family could write a book about my faults, but of course they would never do that!
—Sister Sidekick

Remember Samson? Although he was very strong physically, he had a weakness for women. First, he met a woman in Timnah, a Philistine city, and persuaded his parents to arrange his marriage with her. They did. When his wife betrayed his confidence, he killed thirty men in Ashkelon. His father-in-law retaliated by giving Samson's wife to another man.

You'll shake your head at Samson's second love (Judges 16). Another love, another betrayal. Oh, Delilah! She was not who she appeared to be; she too was conniving. How do we know? When the Philistine rulers offered her large sums of money to find out the secret of Samson's strength so that they could overpower him, she accepted the bribe, knowing their intent.

Yes, scripture tells us she nagged and cried. She probably used every female trick in the book to get the information out of him. He did not realize that she was actually selling him out to the enemy. He did not see the darkness in the heart of his lover that would allow her to betray him in such a horrible way. He evidently lived with her, yet he did not know her. He had no clue as to why she kept asking for the source of his strength.

Love can be blind. The more we care for someone the more we are blind to their faults. If we truly want to see ourselves from all angles, we must be willing to listen to more than one view. Husbands or longtime friends might be a great place to start, but we may need more, like using a three-way mirror. We may be willing to see the front and sides of ourselves, but are we brave enough to look at the view from the back? Remember, others already have that view. We are the only ones who must work to see that aspect of ourselves.

Why do you do this to me? I just want to see the best parts! I'm gonna look on the count of three: 1 . . . 2 . . . —Sister Sidekick

Evaluate Your Image

If a fellow Christian came to you and pointed out some sin she saw in your life, how would you react?

- Would you be humble and appreciative?
- Would you be angry and offended?
- Would you try to justify your actions?
- Would you be hurt?
- Would you pray about the information?
- Would you attempt to make a change?

Give serious consideration to the following questions as you go about your week. Pursue the goal to see the whole picture. Be honest with yourself for the next seven days. Then come next week willing to truly look at who you are.

❋ Is it possible to fool those around us into believing that we are someone we are not? Why or why not?

✳ Can others see things (good or bad) in us that we do not see? Defend your answer.

_____

_____

✳ List three news-grabbing headlines in which someone thought to be perfect was exposed as leading a double life.

_____

_____

_____

- How did the public react?

- How was the guilty person able to hide the truth from so many when her life was so public?

- How did the guilty person react to the revelation?

- How did her reaction affect the public's "new" opinion of her?

Every tree is known by its own fruit. For men do not gather figs from thorns, nor do they gather grapes from a bramble bush.

—Luke 6:44

Love Spans the Years and the Miles
Imogene and Wilburta

Imogene and I have known one another since age thirteen. During high school we spent most weekends together. Imogene introduced me to the Methodist church, but later I found the church of Christ and made my lifetime commitment.

We married shortly after graduating, and I moved to the north side of Kansas City and Imogene lived on the south side. We had children and saw one another less often. I prepared all the flowers for both her children's weddings, and later for her daughter's funeral. She and her husband helped us rebuild a storm-damaged screened-in porch. We vacationed together.

Then a few years ago, I moved to Louisiana. I got a call one day that Imogene had been diagnosed with pancreatic cancer and was having chemo. Pneumonia and a staph infection developed. I left home and cared for her for three weeks. Later when she was recovering from pancreatic surgery, I returned to Missouri for another five weeks to help as needed. We are old and I am not able to do much, but I can pray, do laundry, cook, be her medicine brain, and fetch items.

People ask me, "Why do you journey so far to be with Imo?" Because I love her! This woman cared for her parents, both her in laws, two cousins, and her own daughter as they were dying, and now there is nobody left to care for her. To say she is a good woman is a gross understatement, but like the rest of us, she needed to be a Christian. After much Bible study, Imo desired to be baptized, and just as soon as the open surgical incision healed, she was baptized into Christ. We continue to pray that she can be a servant for many years to come because we want to be side-by-side friends for a long time!

—Wilburta Arrowood, Louisiana

A Tale of Two Sins

For I acknowledge my transgressions, and my sin is always before me.

—Psalm 51:3

♪♫ Song ♫♪

I Bring My Sins to Thee

Pledge

I do hereby pledge to begin each Bible study with prayer.

I will ask God to open my heart to the suffering and struggles of others, to give me courage to admit my own faults, to ask for help, and to keep anything I hear during these classes in the strictest of confidence.

I pledge not only to give advice but also to take it.

I pledge to seek out the counsel of an older person and to give respect to those women who have walked the path before me.

I pledge to do all of these things humbly and in a manner that gives glory to God.

I believe over the years I have been guilty of not fully seeing who I am. Just as I have tried to control what I see in the mirror, I have also tried to control what others see in me as a Christian. Of course both are futile; I am the only one getting fooled here! Oh, I know why I do it. Just like Sister Sidekick said, "Getting real about our own sin can be frightening."

Review the last section of last week's lesson to prepare for a self-evaluation. Remember, we serve an awesome, loving God. He sent Christ to die for our sins, but we must constantly fight the flesh to walk in the light with Christ. Yes, we are saved by His blood, but every day we must choose not only how we live but also how we handle the mistakes that we make. In other words, what we do when we are faced with our own sin.

A Different View: You Lack One Thing

Let's look at two examples from scripture of those who were shown their sin; two very different stories and two very different outcomes.

> Now as He was going out on the road, one came running, knelt before Him, and asked Him, "Good Teacher, what shall I do that I may inherit eternal life?" So Jesus said to him, "Why do you call Me good? No one is good but One, that is, God. You know the commandments: 'Do not commit adultery,' 'Do not murder,' 'Do not steal,' 'Do not bear false witness,' 'Do not defraud,' 'Honor your father and your mother.'" And he answered and said to Him, "Teacher, all these things I have kept from my youth." Then Jesus, looking at him, loved him, and said to him, "One thing you lack: Go your way, sell whatever you have and give to the poor, and you will have treasure in heaven; and come, take up the cross, and follow Me." But he was sad at this word, and went away sorrowful, for he had great possessions (Mark 10:17–22).

Jesus was not angry with this man. He did not use the strong rebukes He had used with the Pharisees. Jesus loved him, but He could see the sin that the man could not see. The Lord had a different view.

The scriptures tell us that the man went away sad—not angry, not rebellious, not defensive, but sad. He did not argue with Jesus, try to bargain, or offer an explanation. That is very interesting. In reality, his wealth was not the issue. What was the real problem? Not money, but the love of money (1 Timothy 6:10).

Wealth is not just a matter of money. To have great wealth is to have great power. Jesus was not just asking this man to become poor. He was actually asking him to give up his wealth and his power.

- As a wealthy man, he had great power; as a follower of Jesus he would be a servant.

- As a wealthy man, he had great comforts; living on the road with Jesus would not be comfortable.

- As a wealthy man, he had friends and family; as a disciple he would leave all of that support system behind.

- As a wealthy man, he had security; as a disciple he would be totally dependent on the Lord to meet all of his daily needs.

A Sin or a Flaw?

He went away sad because he could not make that dramatic change. He believed himself to be a good man already. After all, he didn't steal, lie, commit adultery, or murder, and he honored his mother and father. To his credit he was the one who approached Jesus. He wanted to know. Look at Mark 10:17. He ran to Jesus and fell on his knees before Him. He called Him "Good Teacher." He was respectful. His inquiry seemed to be an honest question from a man really trying to do what was right.

How many of us are walking around believing ourselves to be "good" when we are carrying sin that we are not even aware of? We do not always see our own sin, because it is a part of who we believe ourselves to be. Instead of considering it a sin, we may feel it is a "personal flaw."

It might look something like this:

- I didn't mean to say that, but I've always had trouble with my tongue.
- Of course I get angry! If you had to walk in my shoes, you would get angry too!
- I don't have time for good works. I'm a busy person!
- I wish I could give to others, but I'm always broke.
- That's just me. I've always been that way. God loves me anyway.

Man, she is steppin' on all my toes!

—Sister Sidekick

The Slippery Steps toward Sin

While there are many sins of which we are fully aware, there are also sins that we cannot see from our point of view. Strangely enough, I believe it is possible to have what we would consider an outlandish over-the-top sin and not fully see it. Why do I think that? If it can happen to someone like King David, it can happen to me.

✿ Read 2 Samuel 11 and write a paragraph describing the event in your journal.

Wow! That is quite a story, isn't it? Every time I read this narrative, I try to put myself in Bathsheba's place. Hollywood has had a field day with this one. I have seen every version possible. According to one version, she went willingly. Yet another version portrays it as almost rape. Regardless of the version, Bathsheba did not belong to King David. Of course, that is the first chapter of this multi-layer tale of sin. Let's review a few of the missteps.

- David had idle time on his hands (2 Samuel 11:1).
- David saw something (someone) he wanted and he took it (vv. 2–4).
- When David realized his actions might be found out, he tried to cover them up (vv. 5–8).
- David used his power as king to try to persuade Bathsheba's husband, a valiant solider, to go against his values (vv. 9–11).
- David manipulated and intoxicated (vv. 12–13).
- David plotted and ordered a murder (vv. 14–24).
- David pretended to be consoling (v. 25).
- David hurt an innocent woman (v. 26).
- David thought his sin was covered, but God was displeased (v. 27).

Now I know that I am not the brightest candle on the cake, but I find myself shaking my head and asking, "Really! David actually thought he could get away with all of that?" How can someone with David's track record do something like that and not feel remorse or recognize the sin and want to repent?

The King Is the Man!

This is David we are talking about here, people. David!

- Anointed as a boy to be king (1 Samuel 16:13).
- Killed Goliath (1 Samuel 17:50).
- Best friend to Jonathan, Saul's son (1 Samuel 18:1).
- Great warrior (1 Samuel 18:30).
- Victim of King Saul, he was chased and forced to live on the run (1 Samuel 20:33).

- Honorable when he had an opportunity to kill Saul in the cave but did not (1 Samuel 24:10).

- A man after God's own heart (Acts 13:22).

I'm confused. If David is such a good guy, why would he do something so terrible and not feel bad about it? —Sister Sidekick

The Parable

Then the Lord sent Nathan to David. And he came to him and said to him: "There were two men in one city, one rich and the other poor. The rich man had exceedingly many flocks and herds. But the poor man had nothing, except one little ewe lamb which he had bought and nourished; and it grew up together with him and with his children. It ate of his own food and drank from his own cup and lay in his bosom; and it was like a daughter to him. And a traveler came to the rich man, who refused to take from his own flock and from his own herd to prepare one for the wayfaring man who had come to him; but he took the poor man's lamb and prepared it for the man who had come to him." So David's anger was greatly aroused against the man, and he said to Nathan, "As the Lord lives, the man who has done this shall surely die! And he shall restore fourfold for the lamb, because he did this thing and because he had no pity." Then Nathan said to David, "You are the man!" (2 Samuel 12:1–7).

Did David See His Sin?

David was king, a warrior. Could it be that he did not see his sin because of who he was? He could have what he wanted when he wanted it and women were no exception. Sleeping with a new lover of his choice was nothing new to him. In that manner, he had chosen wives and concubines (2 Samuel 5:13). Death was also nothing new. He had killed many men in battle. War was messy. However, God's laws pertain to us all.

❋ In Nathan's parable, who is represented by the ewe lamb?

❋ What was the injustice that angered King David?

❋ What punishment did David believe the greedy rich man should suffer for taking the poor man's lamb?

❋ What emotion was lacking in the offender that truly angered King David?

Hey, I would be angry too! Why did that rich guy steal from the poor guy? That's not fair!
—Sister Sidekick

The lives of David and Bathsheba are familiar to most of us. We studied the rich young ruler's sin and his reaction.

If I were a person who rated sin, I believe I would say David's transgression was far greater than that of the rich young ruler. Thankfully, we know through our study of scripture that God does not rate sin. Is the sin really the issue? The sobering fact is that the difference between life and death rests squarely with our ability to acknowledge our sins and deal with them appropriately.

We have studied David's sin. In the next lesson, we will look at how David dealt with his sin.

Two Rooms and a Path
Glenna and Carol

Before I was born, my parents moved from a house that had three bedrooms and a bath in an Oklahoma town to a house in the Californian countryside with two rooms and a path. My first memories are the house with two rooms and a path. That was 1937.

They adopted baby Glenna in 1939, and seven years later, "Surprise!" I joined them on the path. I'm not sure when I learned that Glenna was adopted, she was always my sister.

Pesky me; I played in Glenna's makeup and read her love letters from that sailor she was going to marry. I was twelve when they married, and I cried myself to sleep thinking, "She will never really know how I love her." I cannot say that we were close in the following years when she lived in Texas, but we always stayed in touch. Distance was harder to cross in those days. Even phone calls were sparse.

Glenna worked for years for an insurance company. When a new boss moved in, he fired my sister. Coincidentally, there was another lady in the office who was married to the preacher at the local church of Christ. When Glenna walked out, she did too. I believe their friendship saved my sister's soul. She was diagnosed with leukemia and returned to the Lord in 2007.

I flew to her side in her final days in 2011. We prayed and sang and reminisced. She is in her heavenly home now, much grander than our beginning two rooms and a path!

—Carol Maddox, Oregon

WEEK TWELVE

Now I See!

Deal bountifully with Your servant, that I may live and keep Your word. Open my eyes, that I may see wondrous things from Your law.

—Psalm 119:17–18

♪♪ Song ♫

Love for All

Pledge

I do hereby pledge to begin each Bible study with prayer.

I will ask God to open my heart to the suffering and struggles of others, to give me courage to admit my own faults, to ask for help, and to keep anything I hear during these classes in the strictest of confidence.

I pledge not only to give advice but also to take it.

I pledge to seek out the counsel of an older person and to give respect to those women who have walked the path before me.

I pledge to do all of these things humbly and in a manner that gives glory to God.

I would have loved to have been a fly on the wall when Nathan hit David between the eyes with the truth: "You are the man!" (2 Samuel 12:7). There was no tact, diplomacy, or concern about hurting David's feelings. David sinned; God was angry. The end.

One moment David was passing a death sentence upon the perpetrator and the next moment he realized that he had just condemned himself. Nathan was very vivid in his description of the price David would pay for his sins. It's not a pretty picture. Clearly, God was not happy.

David had to deal with the exposed sin. He could have gotten angry, tried to justify his actions, or made excuses. He could have even walked away sad as the rich young ruler did. Following God is always a choice. What did David do?

> *So David said to Nathan, "I have sinned against the Lord."*
> —2 Samuel 12:13

That was all David said. Can you believe it? He admitted his guilt. God knew David's heart was convicted and penitent. David later penned these words, "I acknowledge my transgressions and my sin is always before me" (Psalm 51:3).

> And Nathan said to David, *"The Lord also has put away your sin; you shall not die. However, because by this deed you have given great occasion to the enemies of the Lord to blaspheme, the child also who is born to you shall surely die."*
> —2 Samuel 12:13–14

Consequences

There was forgiveness, but there were also consequences.

Have you ever sympathized with Bathsheba's experiences as this event unfolded? Did she really want to submit to the king? Did she want to marry him? Did she love and grieve for her husband Uriah? Was she the cause of any of David's sins? Was she deeply hurt by his sin? Did she suffer consequences other than the loss of her baby boy? Bathsheba was swept along, side by side in David's sin. We do not read of her choices.

That's the way it is with sin. Just because we do not see it or acknowledge it, does not mean it will not hurt those around us.

✸ Write the consequences that God promised David.

2 Samuel 12:10. The _____ would never depart from David's house.

2 Samuel 12:11. God would raise up _____ from David's house and his _____ would be taken from him.

2 Samuel 12:14. David and Bathsheba's _____ would die.

Aren't we thankful that the Bible never conceals the faults of its noblest men?

This lesson is sad. Can we talk about something else now, please? How about shoes? I like shoes.

—Sister Sidekick

Open Your Eyes

Okay, so here is the good news. Yes, David sinned but that is not the end of the story. When David was shown his sin, he took ownership of it and repented. It is not the sin that determines the end of the story. It is our reaction to the revealing of the sin that is most important.

Our section is titled "The Sin No One Confesses." Do you know what that is? Well, do you? Have you figured it out? Did you think it was one particularly dark sin? Maybe it was some obscure sin?

Nope. The sin that no one confesses is *the sin that we do not see!* If we do not see it, we cannot confess it. If we cannot confess it, we cannot be forgiven. Also, there is no way we can make the needed changes in our lives to prevent that sin from happening again.

I knew the answer all along! I just didn't want to spoil the surprise! —Sister Sidekick

I have saved this lesson for the end of our series for a reason. It is my prayer that by now friendships are formed and bonds created that will allow you to help one another through the difficult task of self-sin awareness. That is not an easy journey. Many of us have become so accustomed to our sin that we are truly not aware that we have it. We need to be told.

As you work with one another, please be kind. Even if your sister wants to see the truth, it might be difficult for her to accept. I meant what I said about being real. I pray that you begin each session by reading the promise and by praying. I pray that you end each session with open hearts and closed mouths!

Oh, I like to talk, but I can keep my mouth shut too! —Sister Sidekick

Open Eyes, Side by Side

My sisters, God brings us together for a reason. We need each other. Love one another. Support one another. Rebuke one another, but always in love. We are stronger together as a family, as a sisterhood, than we could ever be alone. God knew that. That is why He created the church.

No one is perfect. Do not allow foolish pride and blindness to take away the blessings God has planned for you. If someone comes to you with a sin concern, consider it deeply. Pray about it. Speak to others you trust. Allow God to open your eyes. Do not go away sad but stand like the king who was a man after God's own heart (Acts 13:22) and admit, "I have sinned." There will always be consequences for sin, but there are multiple blessings once the sin is acknowledged, confessed, repented of, and forgiven.

Look Like Your Father

Just as my physical body has changed to look more like my mother and father, my spiritual body should mature as well. When others see my spirit, I want them to see Jesus' hands and feet—hands serving and feet willing to go where I am needed. I want them to see a strong back ready to help others carry their burdens, not one curved from old age. When they see me from their perspective, I want them to be able to say, "You look just like your Father!"

The things which are impossible with men are possible with God.

—Luke 18:27

Forgiven Sinners

This will not happen automatically. I must be willing to look honestly at myself from both my view and yours. I must also be willing to give up my power and become a servant. I must humble myself, say I have sinned, ask for forgiveness, and work through the consequences that sin will bring. It is not easy, but it is possible (Luke 18:27).

I believe that it all begins with getting real. So ladies, let's all get real about our own sins. If we are going to see both views, we will need the help of our fellow Christian women. Can I count on you to help me? Do you love me enough to tell me what you really see?

"But rise and stand on your feet; for I have appeared to you for this purpose, to make you a minister and a witness both of the things which you have seen and of the things which I will yet reveal to you. I will deliver you from the Jewish people, as well as from the Gentiles, to whom I now send you, to open their eyes, in order to turn them from darkness to light, and from the power of Satan to God, that they may receive forgiveness of sins and an inheritance among those who are sanctified by faith in Me."

—Jesus, Acts 26:16–18

* Is it possible to be completely unaware of your sin? Why or why not?

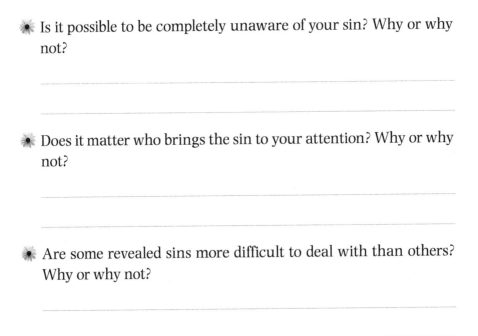

* Does it matter who brings the sin to your attention? Why or why not?

* Are some revealed sins more difficult to deal with than others? Why or why not?

✳ Give an example of someone in scripture besides David who had personal sin revealed to them. How did they react? What was the short-term result of that revelation? What was the long-term result?

_____

_____

_____

✳ Which is more important, the initial reaction of the revealing of sin, or the long-term one? Why?

_____

_____

✳ If you could choose, who would you want to tell you about your unseen sin? Why?

_____

_____

✳ Is it a good idea to have an agreement with one individual to help you see your sin, or should it be the job of all Christians to monitor each other? Why?

_____

_____

PART 5

Celebrate and Reflect

STRENGTH FOR THE ROAD AHEAD

Letters to Cherish
Shirley, Betty, and Mary

December 14, 1967. The date was stamped on the airmail in my hand. It was in my mom's handwriting, addressed to her younger sister, Mary. My aunt found it and mailed it to me as a keepsake. Mom was twenty-four years old with a two-year-old daughter, Pam (that's me) and a four-month-old son, Keith. Our family was living in Japan on an Air Force base, hundreds of miles across the ocean from home.

My mom and her sisters had a special closeness that time and distance couldn't deteriorate. Even though the new-fangled Internet eventually made staying in contact easier and faster, Mom and her sisters kept corresponding regularly by letter.

Growing up as little girls on a farm in Baker, Florida, in the 1940s and '50s, the little sisters had plenty of sunshine, love, work, adventure, and, mischief.

My gentle grandmother loved her girls and faithfully took them to worship where three little girls sat side by side in a small, close-knit congregation that included relatives.

As the sisters each grew up, got married, and left home, they never lost sight of each other.

On February 1, 2017, my mom died unexpectedly. Shock and grief rocked our family. I can still hear Aunt Shirley's sobs, "She was my very best friend; what will I do without her?"

We left her hospital bedside having said goodbye "to the dearest on earth." Weary from the long and emotional night, we tried to rest at her home. Dad walked out to the mailbox and returned with mail. Without a word, he handed me a card; it was from Aunt Mary.

Mom and her sisters have a continuing bond—one that even death cannot break. Thankfully they will all be reunited side by side in heaven.

—Pam Steward, Mississippi

Travel Along, Singing a Song!

The Lord bless you and keep you;
The Lord make His face shine upon you,
And be gracious to you;
The Lord lift up His countenance upon you,
And give you peace.

 —Numbers 6:24–26

Song

When We All Get to Heaven

Pledge

I do hereby pledge to begin each Bible study with prayer.

I will ask God to open my heart to the suffering and struggles of others, to give me courage to admit my own faults, to ask for help, and to keep anything I hear during these classes in the strictest of confidence.

I pledge not only to give advice but also to take it.

I pledge to seek out the counsel of an older person and to give respect to those women who have walked the path before me.

I pledge to do all of these things humbly and in a manner that gives glory to God.

Congratulations! You did it. For several weeks you listened to me teach, preach, whine, question, tease, and confess. I pray that the time you spent with each other studying the word of God has given you a new perspective on side-by-side Christianity. I pray that you have grown closer to God and to one another and that you will continue to support and love each other long after this study is complete.

So far I have done most of the talking. Now it is your turn. Let's look back at our time together and evaluate it using these simple steps.

- Divide the topics of the four main parts of the book among your group. Work in four teams. If there are fewer than four women, it will be necessary for some of you to take more than one topic. Remember, each topic has three weeks of study within.

  1. Through All Kinds of Weather: *Survival*

  2. When Abnormal Becomes Normal: *Chronic Illness*

  3. Lions, Tigers, and Bears—Oh My!: *Fear, Depression, and Other Normal Emotions*

  4. The Sin No One Confesses: *Invisible Faults*

- Each team is to review the lesson prior to your meeting time and come prepared to review the lesson with the rest of the class using the questions provided below.

- Allow comments and questions about each of the four topics.

- As always, begin your time by reviewing the pledge and in prayer. Then switch gears—make this class fun. This is the day to celebrate weeks of time spent with God and your sisters in Christ.

✳ What was the name of your three-part topic?

✳ Briefly retell the storm example used at the beginning of the lesson.

_____

_____

✳ What was used as the biblical example for this lesson?

_____

✳ What scripture or scriptures do you feel best represent your topic?

_____

✳ Did the three weeks of study help you consider this topic in a new way? Did you have an "aha" moment? If so, please share with the group. (Note: This might have been caused by some nugget in the book or by a comment from the group during study.)

✳ Was there anything not said or covered that you would like to talk about now?

_____

✳ Have there been or will there be any changes in your life due to this lesson? If so, name one.

_____

✳ Do you plan to share what you have learned with anyone? If so, who?

_____

✳ Has studying this subject changed how you feel about yourself, God, or others? Please explain.

_____

_____

❋ What is your favorite scripture from the three weeks studying your subject? Why?

_____

_____

Now that the lessons have been thoroughly covered, it is time to talk to each other. Please use these discussion questions to begin your conversation. Of course you are not limited to these questions: I just wanted to give you a jumping-off spot. I've bossed you around enough. You conduct this part of the session in the manner that best suits your group.

❋ Whose story surprised you the most? Why?

_____

_____

❋ What strengths or qualities do you admire most about the women in this room?

_____

_____

❋ Is there anyone in the room whom you would like to thank for sharing a difficult story with the group? Why did this story affect you so deeply?

_____

_____

❋ Do you feel less alone or vulnerable today than you have in the past? Why or why not?

_____

_____

How has this Bible study affected your relationship with God, including your prayer life?

How has this study affected your view of yourself?

Will this new knowledge change your daily walk as a Christian woman? Why or why not?

Well, that's it! We're done. Thank you for allowing me to walk along beside you as we traveled this path together. I have said it before and I will say it again: God never intended for us to walk alone.

Yes, He is always with us, but He provided a support system here on earth. Women need women. I am so thankful for you, my sisters. May God richly bless you as you travel this road called life. May He use us all to bring others to Him. May we support, love, and pray for one another.

None of us are perfect, but we are family, God's family. I love you, my sisters. Until we meet again!

CPSIA information can be obtained
at www.ICGtesting.com
Printed in the USA
FFHW01n0027240918

9 781945 127090